JN083437

海を渡った故郷の味

新装版

認定NPO法人
難民支援協会 編著

Flavours Without Borders

new edition

www.flavours-without-borders.jp

はじめに

故郷エチオピアにいる母から、
時々、母のドレスを送ってもらっています。
「洗わずに送って」と必ず伝えます。
それは、服に残った母の匂いから、
母のこと、故郷のことを思い出すことができるから。

これは、日本にいる難民の方から聞いた話です。

家庭料理の味や匂いの記憶は、生まれ育った土地の記憶を呼び起こすもの。
それは、母国から逃れてきた難民にとって迫害という過酷な経験を想起するものかもしれません。しかし、共に料理を囲んだ大切な人たちとの思い出も、その記憶にはつまっています。

本書は、日本にも迫害から逃れてきた難民が暮らしていることを、もっと多くの方に知っていただきたいという思いから生まれました。収録されているレシピは、すべて、日本にいる難民の方から教えていただいたもの。アジア、中東、アフリカの15の国・地域出身の方々とともに作りました。
日本には、すでに多くの難民の方が暮らしています。
たとえば、故郷の家族に託した幼い子どもに再会する日を願いながら、日本でひとり難民認定を待つカメルーン出身の女性。軍事政権による迫害から単身で日本に逃れ、今は家族と日本で暮らすミャンマー（ビルマ）出身の男性。様々な理由で母国を逃れざるを得ない難民がいます。
紹介する料理の中には、家族が送ってくれるスパイスを使い、故郷の味を再現するようなレシピもあれば、長年の日本での生活を経て変化していったレシピもあります。本書を通じて、料理を味わいながら、その国・地域、そして日本で暮らす難民の姿に思いを寄せていただければ幸いです。なお、この本の収益の一部は、日本に暮らす難民のための支援活動に活用されます。
本書は、2013年に出版されてからたいへん多くの方に読んでいただき、難民の故郷の味を大学の学食で提供する活動が生まれるなど、難民への共感が広がっています。
一方で、日本で難民として認定される方の数は依然として少なく、多くの方が厳しい状況に置かれています。現状を打開するためにはさらに多くの方の理解と支援が欠かせないなかで、レシピの内容はそのままに、このたび新装版を出版することとなりました。
旧版を制作するにあたり全面的なご協力をくださったマッコーリー・グループ・ジャパンの皆さま、新装版出版の機会を与えてくださった株式会社トゥーヴァージンズの皆さまをはじめ、多くの方がお力をくださったことにあらためて感謝いたします。
レシピを教えてくださった難民の方々に心から感謝するとともに、日本に逃れた難民の方々が一日も早く、大切な人たちと料理を囲める日が来ることを願ってやみません。

認定NPO法人　難民支援協会
2020年2月

Foreword

"I sometimes ask my mother to send me her
dresses from home, and whenever I do, I ask her
not to wash them, so that the scent of her dresses
will help remind me of her and
the memories of my homeland."

This is a quote from a refugee in Japan.

Although refugees' memories may sometimes be haunted by experiences of oppression, the aroma and taste of their native dishes evoke memories of home and important people in their lives.

This book is dedicated to those who have taken refuge in Japan. The purpose of this book is to raise awareness to a greater audience about their stories. In this book, there are recipes shared by refugees from 15 countries and regions in Asia, the Middle East and Africa.
Many refugees and people seeking asylum are living in Japan.
For example, a woman from Cameroon who - while waiting to be approved for refugee status in Japan - hopes to see her young children left behind with her family in Cameroon. A Burmese man who escaped persecution from the military regime arrived in Japan alone. Unable to return to his native land, he is building a new life here with his family. Refugees are forced to leave their homeland for reasons beyond their control.
Some of the recipes in the book are a close reproduction of the refugees' taste of home, made using spices sent from their country. Some have been adjusted through their time spent in Japan. We hope to provide the opportunity for those who take this book in hand to send their thoughts by tasting the food introduced here. Part of the proceeds from the book will be used to support refugees living in Japan.
Since being published in 2013, this book was enjoyed by many people, and led to many movements such as Japanese universities and students offering these tastes of faraway home in their cafeterias. This has helped raise awareness and empathy for refugees.
Meanwhile, they continue to struggle as the Japanese government grants refugee status to so few applicants. To assist these refugees, we need even more support and understanding from the public. That is why we decided to republish this cook book.
We give our deepest gratitude to Macquarie Group Japan for their support as well as many others who helped with the production of this book when we first published in 2013, and to Two Virgins Co., Ltd. who gave us the opportunity to publish the new edition. Last but not least, we'd like to express our appreciation for the refugees who shared these recipes with us. We hope that refugees are reunited with their loved ones soon and are able to enjoy these familiar dishes together.

Japan Association for Refugees

February, 2020

マッコーリー・グループは拠点をもつ各国々において積極的に社会貢献を目指しており、マッコーリー・グループ・ジャパンでは、この度、このような本の出版に携わる機会を得られたことを光栄に思っております。

昨年、弊社グループの社員は、東日本大震災直後に見せたチームワーク、その後の復興支援活動に対し、社内表彰制度にて評価を受け、表彰されることとなりました。現在も、多くの社員が復興支援活動を続けております。

弊社グループでは、この受賞による寄付金の一部を難民支援協会と共に作成した本書の制作費にあてさせていただきました。日本にいる難民の認知向上、協会の活動に対する理解を深めていただけるだけでなく、読者の皆さまにも楽しんでいただける一冊に仕上がりました。

私たちは、このような形で日本に庇護を求める難民への支援を通じて地域社会に貢献できたことを光栄に思います。

マッコーリー・グループ・ジャパン

アーサー　尾関

（※こちらは2013年発行時に頂戴したメッセージです）

Macquarie Group continuously seeks ways to actively participate in the communities where it operates around the world, and Macquarie Group Japan is delighted to be a part of the publication of this cookbook.

Last year, the staff at Macquarie Group Japan were collectively recognised by the organisation's firm-wide internal award committee for their teamwork, collaboration, resilience and overall outstanding efforts after the 2011 Great East Japan Earthquake. Many of the staff also continue to help in rebuilding the region in the aftermath of the disaster.

The staff also decided to share a portion of that award to help fund the Japan Association for Refugees through the creation of a cookbook which we hope will raise awareness of the association and its activities, and also bring joy to readers.

We are thankful to be able to assist in this way and to help the Japan Association for Refugees through its excellent work with refugees seeking asylum in Japan and the community.

Arthur Ozeki

Macquarie Group Japan

(*The above message was recieved in 2013.)

MACQUARIE

目次

Table of Contents

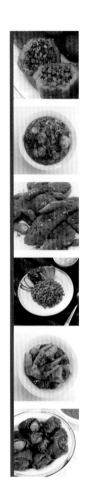

牛肉料理

ライス／麺料理

デザート

換算表

小さじ1＝5㎖
大さじ1＝15㎖
1カップ＝200㎖
30g＝1oz
30㎖＝1floz
454g＝1lb

BEEF

RICE/NOODLES

DESSERT

CONVERSION CHART

1tsp=5ml
1tbsp=15ml
1cup=200ml
30g=1oz
30ml=1floz
454g=1lb

Spicy Salad
with Garlic and Herbs

ニンニクと香味野菜のスパイシーサラダ

Chin
───
チン

材料〔4人分〕

セロリ（みじん切り）	1本
ニンニク（みじん切り）	1かけ
ショウガ（みじん切り）	1かけ
塩	小さじ1
タマネギ（みじん切り）	2個
青唐辛子（輪切り）	2本〔お好みで〕
トマト（くし切り）	3個

Ingredients (Serves 4)

1 celery, minced
1 garlic clove, minced
1 piece ginger, minced
1 tsp salt
2 onions, minced
2 green chillies, chopped (optional)
3 tomatoes, cut into wedges

From the cook

左の写真の布は、首から垂らして着るチン民族の伝統的な衣装の一つです。男性は白と赤い生地（写真左）、女性は緑と赤い生地（p.84）をまといます。今では変わりましたが、昔は、刃を研ぐのが男性の仕事だったため、切れ味が鋭い包丁を持つ男性が良い結婚相手の条件でした。女性の場合は、薪集めを担っていたため、広い林を有していることだったそうです。

The fabric in the left picture is a traditional scarf worn by the Chin people. White and red scarves are worn by men and red and green ones by women (p.84). Times have changed, but in the past, sharpening a knife was a man's task. In order to find their right partner, women had to check the sharpness of a knife at a man's home. Men had to see how large a forest the woman's family owned as women were in charge of collecting wood.

作り方

1. セロリ、ニンニク、ショウガをすり鉢でつぶして塩をまぶし、タマネギ、青唐辛子を加えてよくまぜる。
2. 皿の真ん中に1を盛りつけ、周りをトマトで飾る。

Directions

1. Pound celery, garlic and ginger in a mortar and mix with salt. Add onions and green chillies and mix.
2. Place in the centre of a plate and garnish with sliced tomatoes.

Refreshing Salad

さっぱり味のカラフルサラダ

Azeri

アゼリ

From the cook

アゼリの料理を4品紹介
してくれた難民の方は、
とても料理好きで、こだ
わりのある方。「料理が
きれいに映るためには白
いお皿が一番」と、撮影
の日には白い大皿を持っ
てきてくれました。母国
から取り寄せた様々なス
パイスも持参し、スパイ
スの作り方や料理への使
い方を話してくれました。

The refugee who
introduced the four Azeri
recipes enjoys cooking
and cares about food. He
believes "white plates
enhance the food" so, he
brought a big white plate
on the day of the photo
shoot. He also brought
various spices sent from
his homeland and shared
with us how some of the
native spices were
produced and used.

材料 （4人分）

レモン汁	大さじ1
オリーブオイル	大さじ4
酢	大さじ2
塩	少々
ニンジン（細切り）	1本
黄パプリカ（細切り）	1個
タマネギ（薄切り）	1個
トマト（角切り）	1個
パセリ（みじん切り）	1束

Ingredients （Serves 4）

1 tbsp lemon juice	
4 tbsp olive oil	
2 tbsp vinegar	
Salt	
1 carrot, cut into thin strips	
1 yellow pepper, cut into thin strips	
1 onion, sliced	
1 tomato, diced	
1 bunch parsley, minced	

作り方

1. レモン汁、オリーブオイル、酢、塩を混ぜる。
2. ボウルに切った野菜と、1のドレッシングを和え、パセリを散らす。

Directions

1. Mix lemon juice, olive oil, vinegar and salt to make the dressing.
2. Place the cut vegetables in a bowl. Add the dressing and mix well.
   Sprinkle with parsley.

Nepali-style Spicy Pickles
Achar

ネパール流ピリ辛漬物

アツァ

Nepal
―――
ネパール

材料（4人分）

キュウリ（4cmの棒状に切る）	4本
塩	大さじ½
すりゴマ（白）	大さじ3
チリパウダー	小さじ2
ターメリックパウダー	小さじ½
レモン汁	大さじ3
赤唐辛子	2本
サラダ油	大さじ3

Ingredients（Serves 4）

4 cucumbers, cut into 4 cm-length sticks	
½ tbsp salt	
3 tbsp ground white sesame	
2 tsp chilli powder	
½ tsp turmeric powder	
3 tbsp lemon juice	
2 red chillies	
3 tbsp salad oil	

From the cook

ターメリックや唐辛子でスパイシーに味付けしたキュウリの漬物。ネパール語では「アツァ」。キュウリ以外に、ゴーヤや大根などの野菜を使ったり、白ゴマを黒ゴマに変えたりして作ることもできます。ネパールでは毎日の食卓に並ぶメニュー。おいしく作るコツは野菜の水気をしっかり絞ること。味がなじんでおいしくなる翌日、翌々日に食べるのがおすすめです。

These spicy pickles called *achar* in Nepali, are seasoned with turmeric and chillies. It can be made with other vegetables such as goya (bitter melon), radishes, and black sesame instead of white. In Nepal, they are part of the daily food. An important tip is to squeeze the excess water from the vegetables well. It is recommended to serve a day or two later, allowing the flavours to blend.

作り方

1. ボウルにキュウリを入れ、塩をふってもみ、30分ほどおいて水気をしっかり絞る。
2. すりゴマ、チリパウダー、ターメリックパウダー、レモン汁を入れ、よく混ぜ合わせ、赤唐辛子をちぎって加える。
3. 小さい鍋でサラダ油を熱し、2の上から注ぎ入れ、混ぜ合わせる。

Directions

1. Place cucumbers in a bowl and rub with salt. Leave for 30 minutes and squeeze out any excess water.
2. Add ground sesame, chilli powder, turmeric powder, lemon juice and mix well. Tear red chillies and also add to the mixture.
3. In a small pan, heat the salad oil until very hot and pour over the cucumbers. Mix well.

Cucumber and Yoghurt Salad

キュウリとヨーグルトのサラダ

Kurd

クルド

From the cook

クルド語で「トラク」と呼ばれる、冷製スープのようなサラダです。作り方はとても簡単。油を使う料理が多いクルドではヨーグルト入りのさっぱりとしたこの料理は欠かせません。主に朝食に食べる人が多く、ミントを添えてさらに爽やかな味わいにすることもできます。

This is an easy-to-prepare salad, called *torak*. The taste of yoghurt is refreshing as many of the Kurdish dishes tend to be oily. Mint can also be added to enhance the refreshing taste.

材料（4人分）

ニンニク（みじん切り）	1かけ
ヨーグルト	450 g
塩	小さじ1
水	½カップ
キュウリ（薄切り）	1本
乾燥パセリ	小さじ1
ミズナ（一口大に切る）	1束
※他の葉野菜でも代用可	

Ingredients（Serves 4）

1 garlic clove, minced
450g plain yoghurt
1 tsp salt
½ cup water
1 cucumber, sliced
1 tsp dried parsley
1 bunch mizuna* (potherb mustard), cut into bite-sized pieces
Or any leaf vegetable

作り方

1. ニンニク、ヨーグルト、塩、水をよく混ぜ合わせる。
2. 1を皿に盛りつけ、その上にキュウリを浮かべるように並べ、パセリを散らす。
3. 皿の縁にミズナを飾りつける。

Directions

1. Mix garlic, yoghurt, salt and water.
2. Pour the yoghurt mixture into a salad plate. Gently float the sliced cucumbers on top and sprinkle with parsley.
3. Garnish the rim of the plate with mizuna.

From the cook

クルド民族の多くは、チグリス、ユーフラテス川の上流地域に暮らしています。これらの川の恵みによる肥沃な大地には広大な農地が広がっており、そこから採れる農作物からは豊かな料理が生まれます。また、大地の恵みである花や果物をモチーフとして生まれたのが、オヤという伝統技術のレース編み（写真上）。たった1本の針から生み出されるオヤは、トルコやクルドの文化として、母から娘へ受け継がれてきました。

Many of the Kurdish people live in the upstream region of the Tigris and the Euphrates. Vast farmlands expand across the fertile ground blessed by these rivers. Agricultural produce harvested in this region has nurtured a rich variety of food. Traditional lace-making, called Oya (as pictured above), has been invented by using as motifs flowers and fruits in this region, which are also the blessing of the fertile ground. Oya lace woven by just a single needle has been inherited from mothers to daughters as Turkish and Kurdish culture.

Shepherd's Salad

羊飼いのサラダ

Kurd

クルド

材料（4人分）

A	サラダ油	大さじ3
	チリパウダー	小さじ2
	レモン汁	大さじ2
	パセリ（みじん切り）	大さじ1
	塩、コショウ	少々
タマネギ（薄切り）		½個
キュウリ（輪切り）		2本
レタス（一口大にちぎる）		4枚
ミズナ（一口大に切る）		2束
※他の葉野菜でも代用可		
ピーマン（一口大に切る）		1個
トマト（一口大に切る）		1個

Ingredients（Serves 4）

A	3 tbsp salad oil
	2 tsp chilli powder
	2 tbsp lemon juice
	1 tbsp parsley, minced
	Salt and pepper
½ onion, sliced	
2 cucumbers, sliced	
4 leaves of lettuce, torn into bite-sized pieces	
2 bunches mizuna* (potherb mustard), cut into bite-sized pieces	
*Or any leaf vegetable	
1 green pepper, chopped	
1 tomato, chopped	

作り方

1. Aを混ぜ合わせる。
2. ボウルに切った野菜を入れ、1のドレッシングと混ぜ合わせる。

Directions

1. Mix A to make the dressing.
2. Place vegetables in a bowl. Pour the dressing and mix well.

Lentil and Tomato Stew

Kurd
クルド

レンズ豆とトマトの あったか煮込みスープ

材料（4人分）

A	レモン汁	大さじ1
	サラダ油	大さじ1
	サルチャ（トマトペースト）	小さじ1
	塩	少々
	水	½カップ
赤レンズ豆		200g
水		8カップ
タマネギ（みじん切り）		½個
ニンニク（みじん切り）		2かけ
サラダ油		大さじ1
パセリ（みじん切り）		大さじ1
塩、コショウ		適量
サルチャ（トマトペースト）(p.63参照)		小さじ1
レモン汁		大さじ1

Ingredients（Serves 4）

A	1 tbsp lemon juice
	1 tbsp salad oil
	1 tsp *salcasi* (tomato paste)
	Salt
	½ cup water
200g red lentils	
8 cups water	
½ onion, minced	
2 garlic cloves, minced	
1 tbsp salad oil	
1 tbsp parsley, minced	
Salt and pepper	
1 tsp *salcasi* (refer to page 63)	
1 tbsp lemon juice	

作り方

1. Aを容器で混ぜ合わせる。
2. 鍋に赤レンズ豆、水5カップ、1を加えて沸騰させ、アクを取りながら10分ほど煮込む。
3. タマネギ、ニンニク、水3カップを加え、強火で20分煮る。
4. 別の小さい鍋にサラダ油、パセリ、塩、コショウを入れ、香りが出たら3に加える。
5. サルチャ（トマトペースト）とレモン汁を加え、10分ほど強火で煮込む。

Directions

1. Mix A in a bowl.
2. In a pot, boil red lentils in 5 cups water and A. Simmer for 10 minutes, skimming off the foam.
3. Add onions, garlic and 3 cups water. Cook on a high heat for 20 minutes.
4. In a small pot, heat oil, parsley, salt and pepper to bring out the aroma. Pour into the lentil mixture.
5. Add *salcasi* (tomato paste) and lemon juice and simmer on a high heat for 10 minutes.

Omelette with
Chinese Chives

トマトと相性抜群　ニラたっぷりの卵焼き

Azeri

アゼリ

材料（4人分）

ニラ（2cm幅にざく切り）	3束
A　ジンジャーパウダー	小さじ1
シナモンパウダー	少々
白コショウ	少々
黒コショウ	少々
カルダモンパウダー	少々
塩	少々
卵	3個
サラダ油	大さじ2
オリーブオイル	大さじ1
トマト（くし切り）	1個

Ingredients（Serves 4）

3 bunches Chinese chives, cut into
　2cm-length pieces
A｜1 tsp ginger powder
　｜Pinch of cinnamon powder
　｜Pinch of white pepper
　｜Pinch of black pepper
　｜Pinch of cardamom powder
　｜Salt
3 eggs
2 tbsp salad oil
1 tbsp olive oil
1 tomato, cut into wedges

From the cook

ニラの栽培が盛んで頻繁に食卓に並ぶというアゼリ地域。多くのスパイスを料理に使うのが特徴です。この料理も、本場では、レイハンという紫バジルの乾燥ハーブ、グズルジュルというバラの花びらを乾燥させたものなど独自のスパイスを香りづけとして使います。

In the Azeri region, Chinese chives are grown in abundance and are often used in home-cooked meals. A characteristic of Azeri cuisine is its use of many types of spices. Unique spices such as *reihan* (dried purple basil) and *gyzylkul* (dried rose petals) are used in many dishes to add aroma.

作り方

1. ニラとAをボウルでよく混ぜたら、溶き卵を入れ、塩で味をととのえる。
2. フライパンにサラダ油とオリーブオイルをひき、1の生地を流し込み、平らにし、中火で焼く。
3. 卵が半熟になったら、フタをして弱火で蒸す。焼き面がきつね色になったら、裏返す。
4. フタをせずに弱火で5分ほど焼いたら、皿に盛りつけ、トマトを生地の上に飾りつける。

Directions

1. Mix chives and A in a bowl. Beat in eggs and salt.
2. Heat both oils in a frying pan and pour the omelette mixture to cover the surface of the frying pan. Cook on a medium heat.
3. When the omelette is half-cooked, cover and reduce to a low heat. When the bottom part becomes brown, flip the omelette.
4. Cook for another 5 minutes on a low heat. Place on a plate and garnish with tomatoes.

Mild Coconut Milk and Cashew Nut Curry

ココナッツミルクとカシューナッツのマイルドカレー

Sri Lanka

スリランカ

材料（4人分）

カシューナッツ	300g
ターメリックパウダー	小さじ1
油	適量
ニンニク（みじん切り）	4かけ
タマネギ（薄切り）	1個
シナモンパウダー	小さじ1
パプリカ（一口大に切る）	½個
A　カレーパウダー 　　（ローストする）	大さじ1
ターメリックパウダー	小さじ1
チリパウダー	小さじ½
ココナッツミルク	3カップ
塩	小さじ1

Ingredients（Serves 4）

300g cashew nuts
1 tsp turmeric powder
Oil for stir-frying
4 garlic cloves, minced
1 onion, sliced
1 tsp cinnamon powder
½ red pepper, cut into bite-sized pieces
A | 1 tbsp curry powder, roasted
　 | 1 tsp turmeric powder
　 | ½ tsp chilli powder
3 cups coconut milk
1 tsp salt

From the cook

スリランカの定番料理であるカレーは、いくつもの具材を一緒に調理はせず、ジャガイモやナス、豆など各具材でそれぞれのカレーを作り、たくさんの種類を食卓へ並べます。この料理はココナッツミルクを加えたマイルドな味わいが特徴。日本でもおなじみのチリやターメリックだけでなく、時にはパンダーナスやカレーの葉を入れ、さらに味に深みをつけることもできます。

Curry is a staple food in Sri Lanka. Unlike Japanese curry, each ingredient, such as potato, aubergine, and beans is prepared as a separate curry. These varieties of curries are served together in the same meal. This dish tastes mildly of coconut milk. It contains not only the well-known spices of chilli and turmeric, but you can also add pandanus leaves or curry leaves to further enhance the flavour.

作り方

1. 鍋にカシューナッツが浸る程度の水を入れ、30分ほどおく。ターメリックパウダー小さじ1を加え、そのまま火にかけカシューナッツがやわらかくなるまで20〜25分ほど茹で、水気を切る。
2. フライパンに油をひき、ニンニクとタマネギを炒める。タマネギが黄金色になったら、シナモンパウダーとパプリカを加えてさらに炒める。
3. Aを加え、焦がさないように気をつけながらさっと炒め、ココナッツミルクを加えて沸騰させる。
4. 茹でたカシューナッツと塩を加え、カシューナッツが見える程度に水分が減るまで煮込む。

Directions

1. In a pot, place cashew nuts and enough water to cover and leave to soak for 30 minutes. Add 1 tsp turmeric powder and boil for 20-25 minutes until the nuts become soft. Drain and place aside.
2. Heat oil in a frying pan and cook garlic and onions. When the onions are golden-brown, add cinnamon powder and red pepper. Continue to cook.
3. Add A, be careful not to burn the powder. Add coconut milk and bring to the boil.
4. Add boiled cashew nuts and salt. Cook until the soup is reduced to bring out the nuts.

Masoor Daal Curry

レンズ豆のカレー

Nepal

ネパール

From the cook

一般にダールカレーというとレンズ豆のカレーと思われがちですが、ダールとは豆という意味でネパールでは様々な種類の豆カレーがあります。豆に加え、肉や野菜を入れることもあります。このレンズ豆を使ったものは「マスールダール」と呼ばれます。レシピを紹介してくれた難民の方はこのカレーをナンと、ピリ辛漬物アツァ（p.14）、豚肉のガラムマサラ炒め（p.42）と一緒に紹介してくれました。

Most people imagine lentils when they think of *daal* curry. However, *daal* simply means beans, and various kinds of beans are used for curry in Nepal. Meat and vegetables can also be added. Curry with lentils is actually called *masoor daal*. The refugee introduced this dish along with naan, Spicy Pickles *Achar* (p.14) and Pork Stir-fry with Garam Masala (p.42).

材料（4人分）

赤レンズ豆	300g
水	5カップ
塩	少々
ターメリックパウダー	小さじ½
ニンニク（みじん切り）	2かけ
ショウガ（みじん切り）	1かけ
油	適量
タマネギ（薄切り）	½個
赤唐辛子	1本

Ingredients（Serves 4）

- 300g red lentils
- 5 cups water
- Salt
- ½ tsp turmeric powder
- 2 garlic cloves, minced
- 1 piece ginger, minced
- Oil for stir-frying
- ½ onion, sliced
- 1 red chilli

作り方

1. 赤レンズ豆はさっと洗って30分ほど水に浸し、ざるに上げて水気を切る。
2. 鍋に赤レンズ豆、水、塩、ターメリックパウダー、半量のニンニク、ショウガを入れ、25分ほど茹でる。水分が少ない場合は水をさらに加える。
3. フライパンに油をひき、残りのニンニクを入れ、香りが出たらタマネギを加える。タマネギが透き通ってきたら赤唐辛子をちぎって加え、こんがりと炒め、2の鍋に入れる。
4. アクを取りながら煮汁が少なくなるまで煮込み、塩で味をととのえる。

Directions

1. Wash red lentils and soak in the water for 30 minutes. Drain.
2. In a pot, add red lentils, water, salt, turmeric powder, half portion of garlic and ginger. Simmer for 25 minutes, add more water if necessary.
3. Heat oil in a frying pan and cook the remaining garlic. Add onions when aromatic. When onions have turned translucent, tear red chilli and add. Pour the contents into the lentil mixture.
4. Continue cooking to reduce the liquid while skimming the foam. Add salt to taste.

Bangladeshi Egg Curry

バングラデシュのエッグカレー

Bangladesh

バングラデシュ

材料（4人分）

タマネギ（薄切り）		2個
トマト（一口大に切る）		2個
ニンニク（みじん切り）		2かけ
ショウガ（みじん切り）		2かけ
油		適量
ゆで卵（粗く切る）		4個
A	ガラムマサラパウダー	小さじ1
	チリパウダー	小さじ1
	ターメリックパウダー	小さじ1
	クミンパウダー	小さじ1
	コリアンダーパウダー	小さじ1
	塩	小さじ1

Ingredients（Serves 4）

2 onions, sliced		
2 tomatoes, chopped		
2 garlic cloves, minced		
2 pieces ginger, minced		
Oil for stir-frying		
4 boiled eggs, coarsely chopped		
A	1 tsp garam masala powder	
	1 tsp chilli powder	
	1 tsp turmeric powder	
	1 tsp cumin powder	
	1 tsp coriander powder	
	1 tsp salt	

From the cook

このレシピを紹介してくれた難民の方は母親がこのカレーを作ってくれた時のことを良く覚えており、思い出を話してくれました。母国では朝昼夜いつでも食べたくなるような人気メニュー。とくに朝は、野菜やピーナッツなどのフライ、ナンと合わせて食べられています。日本米やパンと合わせてもおいしくいただけます。

The refugee who introduced this recipe remembers well how his mother used to cook this curry for him and shared his story with us. It is a popular dish in Bangladesh, eaten throughout the day. Especially for breakfast, people eat this curry with fried vegetables, peanuts and naan. It also goes well with Japanese rice or bread.

作り方

1. 鍋に油をひき、タマネギ、トマト、ニンニク、ショウガを炒める。
2. 別の鍋で、粗く切ったゆで卵とAを炒め合わせ、1に入れて弱火でじっくり煮込む。

Directions

1. Heat oil in a pot and cook onions, tomatoes, garlic and ginger.
2. In a separate pot, cook the chopped boiled eggs and A. Add to the tomato mixture and stew thoroughly.

Steamed Fish in Spicy Tomato Sauce

トマト味のピリ辛蒸し魚

Uganda

──────

ウガンダ

材料 （4人分）

ティラピア	4尾
※鯛などの白身魚でも代用可	
油	適量
トマト （ざく切り）	2個
ホールトマト	½缶（200g）
タマネギ （薄切り）	½個
青唐辛子 （輪切り）	1個
カレーパウダー	小さじ2
塩	小さじ1
水	¾カップ

Ingredients （Serves 4）

4 tilapia*	
Or other white fish such as porgy	
Oil for stir-frying	
2 tomatoes, chopped	
½ tin (200g) whole tomatoes	
½ onion, sliced	
1 green chilli, chopped	
2 tsp curry powder	
1 tsp salt	
¾ cup water	

From the cook

ウガンダでは、グリーンバナナを葉で包んで茹で、ペースト状にしたものや、キャッサバ（タピオカの原料）やポショ（トウモロコシ粉を煮たもの）が主食です。最近では若い世代を中心に、主食として米も人気になってきました。海はありませんが、アフリカ最大の湖、ビクトリア湖に接していることからティラピアなどの川魚が流通しています。日本では通販や上野のアメ横などで手に入ります。

In Uganda, boiled and mashed green bananas, as well as *Cassava* (raw ingredient for tapioca) or *posho* (boiled maize flour) are the main staple foods. Today, rice is becoming popular among younger Ugandans. The country is landlocked but is home to Lake Victoria, Africa's largest lake. For this reason, river fish such as tilapia are commonly used in Ugandan cooking. In Japan, you can buy tilapia through mail order or at the Ameyoko market in Ueno.

作り方

1. 魚は頭と尾を切って、内臓を取り水洗いし、ぶつ切りにする。
2. 鍋に油をひき、トマト、ホールトマト、タマネギを加え、タマネギがしんなりするまで、トマトをつぶしながら炒める。
3. 鍋に魚を加え、青唐辛子、カレーパウダー、塩、水を加える。フタをして、途中何度か返しながら弱火で10〜15分煮る。

Directions

1. Cut heads and tails off the fish, remove the guts and wash. Cut into large chunks.
2. Heat oil in a pot, add chopped tomatoes, whole tomatoes and onions. Mash whole tomatoes in the pot and cook until onions become translucent.
3. Place the fish in the pot. Add green chillies, curry powder, salt and water. Cover and cook on a low heat for 10-15 minutes while turning the fish over a few times.

Spinach and Fish in Peanut Butter Soup

ホウレンソウと魚のピーナッツバタースープ

D.R. Congo

コンゴ
民主共和国

材料（4人分）

棒ダラ	1尾
※生のアジ4尾等でも代用可 5分ほど下茹でする。	
ホウレンソウ（ざく切り）	1束
水	3½カップ
油	適量
タマネギ（薄切り）	1個
ナス（薄切り）	2個
ピーマン（縦に細切り）	1個
固形ブイヨン	1個
ホールトマト	½缶（200g）
ナツメグパウダー	少々
ピーナッツバター（無糖）	大さじ3
塩	少々

Ingredients （Serves 4）

1 dried and salted cod*

or other fresh fish, such as 4 horse mackerel, boiled for 5 minutes.

1 bunch spinach, chopped	
3½ cups water	
Oil for stir-frying	
1 onion, sliced	
2 aubergines, sliced	
1 green pepper, sliced lengthways	
1 bouillon cube	
½ tin (200g) whole tomatoes	
Pinch of ground nutmeg	
3 tbsp unsweetened peanut butter	
Salt	

From the cook

コンゴ民主共和国では川魚、海水魚問わず干し魚がよく料理に用いられます。そのためこの料理はとてもポピュラーで、主食であるイモ類などと一緒に食べることが一般的。ピーナッツバターもおなじみの食材で、魚料理にだけでなく鶏肉や豚肉料理にも使用されます。

In the Democratic Republic of the Congo (D.R. Congo), dried river and sea fish is often used in cooking. It is a popular dish and is often served with potatoes, a staple ingredient in Congolese cuisine. Peanut butter is also a common ingredient and can be used in chicken and pork dishes.

作り方

1. 魚はやわらかくなるまで10分ほど茹で、食べやすい大きさにほぐす。ホウレンソウも、別の鍋でさっと茹で、水気を切る。
2. 魚とホウレンソウを鍋に入れ、水3カップを加えて沸騰するまで火にかける。
3. フライパンに油をひき、タマネギ、ナス、ピーマンを炒め、固形ブイヨン、ホールトマト、ナツメグパウダーを加える。タマネギに火が通ったら、水½カップを足し、煮立たせる。
4. 3を2に入れ、ピーナッツバターと塩を加えて弱火にし、3分ほど煮込む。

Directions

1. Boil the dried fish for 10 minutes or until it becomes soft, and crumble into bite-sized pieces. In a separate pot, blanch the spinach and drain.
2. Put the boiled fish and spinach in a pot with 3 cups water and bring to the boil.
3. Heat oil in a frying pan and cook onions, aubergines and green pepper. Add bouillon cube, whole tomatoes and ground nutmeg. When the onions turn translucent, add ½ cup water and bring to the boil.
4. Pour the vegetable mixture into the fish mixture. Add peanut butter and salt, mix well and cook on a low heat for 3 minutes.

Stir-fried Fish and Vegetables with Sweet Potatoes

アジと野菜の炒めもの　サツマイモ添え

材料（4人分）

アジ	4尾
ナツメグパウダー	少々
塩	少々
油	適量
タマネギ（薄切り）	½個
ピーマン（縦に細切り）	1個
パプリカ（オレンジや赤、縦に細切り）	2個
A　固形ブイヨン	1個
ジンジャーパウダー	小さじ½
ニンニク（すりおろす）	2かけ
レモン汁	大さじ2
水	1¼カップ
サツマイモ（一口大に切る）	4個
固形ブイヨン	1個
バター	30g

Ingredients （Serves 4）

4 horse mackerels	
Ground nutmeg	
Salt	
Oil for frying/stir-frying	
½ onion, sliced	
1 green pepper, sliced lengthways	
2 orange/red peppers, sliced lengthways	
A　1 bouillon cube	
½ tsp ginger powder	
2 garlic cloves, grated	
2 tbsp lemon juice	
1¼ cups water	
4 sweet potatoes, cut into bite-sized pieces	
1 bouillon cube	
30g butter	

作り方

1. 内臓を取り水洗いしたアジの胴に切り込みを入れ、半分に切る。全体にナツメグパウダーと塩をまぶす。
2. 鍋に油を熱し、アジに火が通るまで揚げる。
3. フライパンに油をひき、タマネギ、ピーマン、パプリカを炒め、十分に火が通ったらA、アジ、水を加えフタをして、10分ほど蒸し焼きにする。
4. 別の鍋にサツマイモと固形ブイヨン1個を入れた湯で茹でる。
5. フライパンにバターを溶かし、茹でたサツマイモとナツメグパウダーを混ぜ、3と一緒に皿に盛りつける。

Directions

1. Remove the guts from the horse mackerels and wash. Make a slit on the side of the fish and cut in half. Sprinkle with ground nutmeg and salt.
2. Fry the fish in oil until thoroughly cooked. Place aside.
3. Heat oil in a frying pan, and cook onions and green/orange/red peppers. Add A, the fried horse mackerels and water. Cover and cook for 10 minutes.
4. Boil sweet potatoes in water with 1 bouillon cube.
5. In a separate frying pan, melt butter on a medium heat. Add the boiled sweet potatoes, and sprinkle ground nutmeg and mix. Serve with the fish mixture.

フランス語が公用語であるコンゴ民主共和国ではサツマイモと魚を意味する「パタットドゥス　オ　ポワソン」が料理名となっています。国土が海に面する部分が少なく、川が多いことから、川魚の方が頻繁に食べられます。レシピを紹介してくれた難民の方も種類にこだわらず、様々な魚を使って料理をしているそうです。レシピでは日本で手に入りやすいアジを使っていますが、他の魚でも作れる夕食の定番メニューです。

In the Democratic Republic of the Congo (D.R. Congo), where French is the official language, this dish is called *Patate douce au Poisson* (sweet potato and fish). River fish is preferred in D.R. Congo because the country has only a few costlines while many rivers flow through the territory. The refugee who shared this recipe enjoys cooking with various types of fish. Although the recipe uses horse mackerel, which is easy to find in Japan, any kind of fish may be used. It is a popular meal served for dinner in D.R. Congo.

Spicy Fried Fish

サンマのスパイシーフライ

Bangladesh

バングラデシュ

From the cook

このレシピを教えてくれた難民の方の得意料理でもある、作り方が簡単で、少ない材料でできるうれしい一品です。海に接し、川や沼が多いバングラデシュでは魚が多く食べられています。この料理もサンマに限らず、様々な魚で調理できます。スパイスが効いた味付けで、ご飯とよく合います。

The refugee who introduced this dish cited it as his personal favourite. You can cook this dish very easily with minimum ingredients. Bangladesh has a vast coastline and an extensive number of rivers and ponds. Thus, fish stands as one of the main ingredients in the country. Though saury is used in this recipe, various other types of fish can also be used. As this dish is strongly seasoned with spices, it goes well with rice.

材料（4人分）

サンマ		4尾
A	ガラムマサラパウダー	小さじ2
	チリパウダー	小さじ2
	ターメリックパウダー	小さじ2
	クミンパウダー	小さじ2
	コリアンダーパウダー	小さじ2
	塩、コショウ	少々
油		適量

Ingredients（Serves 4）

4 saury		
A	2 tsp garam masala powder	
	2 tsp chilli powder	
	2 tsp turmeric powder	
	2 tsp cumin powder	
	2 tsp coriander powder	
	Salt and pepper	
Oil for frying		

作り方

1. サンマは内臓を取り水洗いし、食べやすい大きさに切る。
2. Aを混ぜ合わせて、サンマにまぶす。
3. 鍋に油を熱し、サンマをこんがりと揚げる。

Directions

1. Remove the guts from the saury and wash. Cut into large bite-sized pieces.
2. Mix A together and rub onto the saury.
3. Fry saury in oil until browned.

Potato and
Fried Fish
in Spicy Stew

ジャガイモと揚げ魚のピリ辛煮込み

Cameroon

カメルーン

材料（4人分）

ジャガイモ	8個
塩	少々
アジ	4尾
チリパウダー	少々
固形ブイヨン（粉末にする）	¼個
A ┌ トマト	4個
│ タマネギ	⅓個
│ 青ネギ	2センチ
│ セロリの葉	⅓束
│ パクチー	1束
│ シシトウ	4個
│ ニンニク	4かけ
└ ショウガ	4かけ
油	適量
タマネギ（薄切り）	¼個
固形ブイヨン	2個

Ingredients（Serves 4）

8 potatoes	
Salt	
4 horse mackerels	
Pinch of chilli powder	
¼ bouillon cube, crushed into powder	
A ┌ 4 tomatoes	
│ ⅓ onion	
│ Scallions, 2cm	
│ ⅓ bunch celery leaves	
│ 1 bunches cilantro leaves	
│ 4 shishito peppers	
│ 4 garlic cloves	
└ 4 pieces ginger	
Oil for frying/stir-frying	
¼ onion, sliced	
2 bouillon cubes	

From the cook

ペーストには青ネギ、セロリの葉、パクチー、シシトウといった香味野菜が入っています。料理を作ってくれた難民の方が、日本に来たばかりの頃、言葉が分からない上に、同じ野菜でも見た目や大きさが違うため、母国で使っていた食材を見つけることが大変だったというエピソードを話してくれました。

This dish contains many kinds of potherbs, such as scallions, celery leaves, cilantro (coriander) leaves and shishito. The refugee who shared this recipe told us how difficult it was for him to find the same vegetables and herbs used in his home country. He obviously couldn't speak or read Japanese, and the shape and size of the vegetables in Japan were different from his homeland.

作り方

1. ジャガイモは塩をまぶし、水分が出てきたら、水気を切る。
2. アジは内臓を取り水洗いし、4つに切り、塩、チリパウダー、つぶした固形ブイヨンをふっておく。
3. フライパンに油を熱し、アジに火が通るまで揚げる。
4. Aを一口大に切り、ミキサーにかけペースト状にする。
5. 鍋に油をひき、タマネギが黄金色になるまで炒める。アジ、ペースト状にしたA、ジャガイモ、固形ブイヨン、塩を加え、ジャガイモに火が通るまで、静かにかき混ぜながら、弱火で煮込む。

Directions

1. Sprinkle potatoes with salt. Leave for a few minutes and wipe off any excess moisture.
2. Remove the guts from the horse mackerels and wash. Chop into 4 pieces and sprinkle with salt, chilli powder and crushed bouillon cube.
3. Fry horse mackerels in oil.
4. Cut A into chunks and blend in a mixer to make a paste.
5. Heat oil in a pot and cook onions until golden-brown. Add fried horse mackerels, paste from A, potatoes, bouillon cubes and salt. Cook on a low heat until the potatoes are thoroughly cooked, stirring occasionally.

Salmon
with Sweet Basil

サケのスイートバジル和え

Karen

カレン

材料（4人分）

サケ	4切れ
片栗粉	適量
塩	少々
味の素	少々
油	適量
タマネギ（みじん切り）	1個
A 味の素	少々
ナンプラー	大さじ1
ニンニク（みじん切り）	3かけ
レモングラス（みじん切り）	3本
ターメリックパウダー	小さじ1
チリパウダー	大さじ1
塩	適量
スイートバジル（みじん切り）	1束

Ingredients（Serves 4）

4 slices of salmon	
Potato starch	
Salt	
Ajinomoto powder	
Oil for frying/stir-frying	
1 onion, minced	
A Ajinomoto powder	
1 tbsp fish sauce, or soy sauce	
3 garlic cloves, minced	
3 lemongrass, minced	
1 tsp turmeric powder	
1 tbsp chilli powder	
Salt	
1 bunch sweet basil, minced	

From the cook

この料理は焼きサケを使ってもおいしくいただけます（写真上）。風味づけに、アジア食材店などで購入できる香辛料バンウコンも入れることもあります。カレン州は川に囲まれている地域で魚介類が多く食べられることもあり、この料理も現地ではナマズやコイなどの川魚を使います。牛角の笛やドラ（写真左）は、カレン民族のシンボル。ドラはお祭りなど人を集める時に鳴らします。

You can use stir-fried salmon instead of frying (as pictured above). The spice *Ban'ukon*, which can be bought at Asian food shops, can also be added to enhance the flavour. Karen State is surrounded by rivers, hence catfish and carp are often used to cook this dish. The buffalo horn and the gong are the symbols of the Karen (as pictured left). The gong is clanged to call people to festivals.

作り方

1. サケは一口大に切り、片栗粉、塩、味の素をまぶす。
2. 鍋に油を熱し、サケを揚げる。
3. フライパンに油をひき、タマネギが黄金色になるまで炒める。Aを加えて混ぜる。
4. 揚げたサケを加え、バジルを散らして軽く混ぜる。

Directions

1. Cut the salmon into bite-sized pieces, sprinkle with potato starch, salt and Ajinomoto powder.
2. Fry salmon in oil.
3. Heat oil in a frying pan, and cook onions until golden-brown. Add A and mix well.
4. Add the salmon, sprinkle with basil and mix.

Shellfish Soup

Karen

カレン

ツブ貝のまろやかスープ

材料（4人分）

米	⅓カップ
油	適量
タマネギ（みじん切り）	1個
A 味の素	少々
ナンプラー	大さじ1
ニンニク（みじん切り）	3かけ
レモングラス（みじん切り）	3本
ターメリックパウダー	小さじ1
チリパウダー	大さじ1
塩	少々
ツブ貝	12個
水	4¼カップ

Ingredients (Serves 4)

⅓ cup uncooked rice	
Oil for stir-frying	
1 onion, minced	
A Ajinomoto powder	
1 tbsp fish sauce, or soy sauce	
3 garlic cloves, minced	
3 lemongrass, minced	
1 tsp turmeric powder	
1 tbsp chilli powder	
Salt	
12 whelks	
4¼ cups water	

From the cook

カレン民族の伝統的なスープで、現地では日常食。調味料とタマネギを混ぜ合わせたものは、サケのスイートバジル和え（p.38）に使ったものと同じです。スープのとろみ付けに使った米の粉はカレン料理ではよく使うので、多めに作って常備しています。

This is a traditional soup prepared by the Karen people almost everyday. The spiced onions used in this recipe also appears in the Salmon with Sweet Basil recipe (p.38). Rice powder which thickens the soup is frequently used in Karen dishes. Thus, the rice powder is usually prepared in advance and preserved.

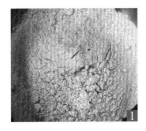

作り方

1. 米をフライパンで乾煎りし、こんがりと焼けたら冷まし、ミキサーにかけ、パウダー状にする。
2. フライパンに油をひき、タマネギが黄金色になるまで炒め、Aを加えてよく混ぜ合わせる。
3. 別の鍋で4カップの湯を沸かし、ツブ貝を茹でる。
4. 3に1を¼カップの水で溶いたものと2を加え、よく混ぜて味をなじませる。

Directions

1. Dry-roast rice in a frying pan until browned, cool, and put in a mixer and ground into a powder.
2. Heat oil in a frying pan and cook the onions until golden-brown. Add A and mix thoroughly.
3. In a different pot, boil the whelks in 4 cups water.
4. Mix the powdered rice with ¼ cup water and add to the pot. Add the onion mixture, mix thoroughly to bring out the flavour.

Pork Stir-fry with Garam Masala

豚肉のガラムマサラ炒め

Nepal

ネパール

材料（4人分）

豚バラブロック（一口大に切る）		350g
油		適量
タマネギ（みじん切り）		¼個
A	ターメリックパウダー	小さじ1
	ガラムマサラパウダー	大さじ1
	チリパウダー	少々
	塩	少々
ニンニク（みじん切り）		1かけ
ショウガ（みじん切り）		1かけ
トマト（一口大に切る）		1個

Ingredients（Serves 4）

350g pork ribs,
　cut into bite-sized pieces
Oil for stir-frying
¼ onion, minced
A | 1 tsp turmeric powder
　| 1 tbsp garam masala powder
　| Chilli powder
　| Salt
1 garlic clove, minced
1 piece ginger, minced
1 tomato, cut into bite-sized pieces

From the cook

この料理の主な味付けは、マサラ、ニンニク、トマト。ネパール料理には欠かせない3つの食材です。今回使用したマサラは、シナモンやナツメグなど様々なスパイスがミックスされたガラムマサラという種類で、作り手によってその種類や配合は異なります。日本では配合済みのものがスーパーで簡単に手に入ります。

The main seasoning used in this dish is masala, garlic, and tomato. These three ingredients are vital in Nepali cuisine. The masala used in this recipe is garam masala, which is a mixture of many types of spices such as cinnamon and nutmeg. The selection of spices and ratios are different, depending on the cook. In Japan, you can purchase readymade garam masala at regular grocery stores.

作り方

1. 豚肉をたっぷりの水で茹でる。
2. フライパンに油をひき、タマネギがしんなりするまで炒め、茹でた豚肉を加える。
3. Aを入れ、よく混ぜ合わせたら、ニンニク、ショウガ、トマトを加え、炒めながら味をなじませる。

Directions

1. Boil the pork in ample water.
2. Heat oil in a frying pan and cook the onions until translucent. Add the boiled pork.
3. Add A and mix well. Then add garlic, ginger, tomato, and continue cooking until the flavours are blended.

Taro Stew

サトイモのさっぱり煮込み

Kachin

カチン

From the cook

カチン料理は、トウガラ
シやニンニク、ショウガ
などをたっぷり使ったス
パイシーなものから、こ
のスープのようなさっぱ
りしたものまでバラエテ
ィに富んでいます。中国
との国境に近いため、中
華料理の影響も受けてお
り、日本でも親しみやす
い味付けです。

Kachin dishes have a
wide variety of flavours,
from spicy dishes that
use plenty of chilli, garlic,
and ginger, to lightly
flavoured dishes like this
soup. As it is located
near the Chinese border,
Kachin cuisine is also
influenced by Chinese
food; thus, making it a
familiar taste to the Japanese.

材料（4人分）

骨付き豚肉、または豚バラ肉	200g
塩	小さじ2
味の素	少々
水	4カップ
サトイモ（茹でて皮をむく）	8個
ブロッコリー（一口大に切る）	½株
カリフラワー（一口大に切る）	½株
チンゲン菜（一口大に切る）	1株
オクラ（一口大に切る）	4本

Ingredients（Serves 4）

200g pork (belly or with the bone),
  sliced

2 tsp salt

Ajinomoto powder

4 cups water

8 taros, boiled and peeled

½ broccoli, cut into bite-sized pieces

½ cauliflower, cut into bite-sized pieces

1 bunch bok choy, cut into bite-sized
  pieces

4 okras, cut into bite-sized pieces

作り方

1. 鍋に豚肉、塩、味の素、水を入れ、煮込む。豚肉がやわらかくなったらサトイモを加
   え10〜15分煮込む。
2. ブロッコリー、カリフラワー、チンゲン菜、オクラを加え、5分ほど煮込む。

Directions

1. Place the pork, salt, Ajinomoto powder and water in a pot. When pork is tender, add
   taros and cook for another 10-15 minutes.
2. Add the vegetables and cook for another 5 minutes.

Tomato Stew with Aubergine and Lentils

ナスとレンズ豆のトマトシチュー

Iran

イラン

材料（4人分）

スペアリブ（骨に沿って切る）	400g
タマネギ（くし型切り）	1個
トマト（ざく切り）	1個
ニンニク（薄切り）	5かけ
トマトペースト	大さじ1
カレーパウダー	小さじ½
塩	小さじ1
水	4カップ
赤レンズ豆	200g
乾燥レモンまたは 生のレモン（半分に切る）	4個
サフラン	少々
バター	30g
ナス（皮をむいて縦に半分に切る）	4本
ジャガイモ（一口大に切る）	3個
塩	適量

Ingredients（Serves 4）

- 400g pork spare ribs, cut along the bones
- 1 onion, cut into wedges
- 1 tomato, chopped coarsely
- 5 garlic cloves, sliced
- 1 tbsp tomato paste
- ½ tsp curry powder
- 1 tsp salt
- 4 cups water
- 200g red lentils
- 4 dried (or fresh) lemons, cut into half
- Pinch of saffron
- 30g butter
- 4 aubergines, peeled and cut into half vertically
- 3 potatoes, cut into chunks
- Salt

From the cook

この料理を紹介してくれた難民の方は豚肉を食べることが禁じられているイスラム教からキリスト教へ改宗しているということで、日本では手に入りやすい豚肉を使って料理をしてくれました。イランではラム肉や牛肉を使うことが多く、人気の定番家庭料理だというこのシチュー。母親の得意料理だったため、子どもの頃に作り方を覚えたそうです。仕事で家を留守にすることが多かった両親のために、自分が代わりに作り、二人を喜ばせることもあったとのこと。母国の思い出がつまった一品です。乾燥レモン（写真上）は通販などで手に入ります。

Since the refugee who shared this recipe has converted from Islam to Christianity, he used pork for this dish which is easier to find in Japan. This stew is a staple home cuisine in Iran and commonly made with lamb or beef. He learnt how to cook this from his mother, as this was her speciality. As a child, he sometimes surprised his parents by cooking this dish for them when they were busy with work. The dish is full of memories of his home country. Dried lemons, as pictured above, can be bought through mail order.

作り方

1. 鍋に豚肉、タマネギ、トマト、ニンニク、トマトペースト、カレーパウダー、塩、水を入れ、45分煮込む。
2. 別の鍋にさっと洗った赤レンズ豆を入れ、十分な水で、やわらかくなるまで15分ほど中火で茹で、ざるに上げておく。
3. 豚肉がやわらかくなったら、赤レンズ豆、乾燥レモン、サフランを加える。乾燥レモンがやわらかくなったら、鍋の中でつぶして果汁を出す。
4. フライパンでバターを熱し、ナスとジャガイモをそれぞれ炒める。
5. ナス、ジャガイモ、塩を豚肉の入った鍋に加え、味がなじむまで煮込む。

Directions

1. Place pork, onions, tomatoes, garlic, tomato paste, curry powder, salt and water in a pot and simmer for about 45 minutes.
2. Rinse red lentils, place in a separate pot with ample water and boil on a medium heat for about 15 minutes or until soften. Drain.
3. When pork is tender, add lentils, dried lemon pieces and saffron. Once the lemons become soft, press them to release the juice.
4. In a frying pan, melt the butter and cook the aubergines and potatoes respectively.
5. Add the aubergines, potatoes and salt to the pork mixture and stew until the flavours are blended.

Mild Chicken Curry

まろやかチキンカレー

Pakistan

パキスタン

材料（4人分）

カシューナッツ	50g
タマネギ（薄切り）	3個

A

オリーブオイル	大さじ2
カルダモン（粒）	小さじ1
クローブ（粒）	小さじ1
ローリエの葉	2枚
黒コショウ（粒）	小さじ1
クミンシード	小さじ1
ニンニクとショウガのペースト	大さじ3

　　※ニンニクとショウガをそれぞれすりつ
　　　ぶし、同じ割合で混ぜ合わせる

ホールトマト	1缶（400g）

B

温めた牛乳	1¼カップ
ミックススパイス	大さじ2

　　※チリパウダー、コリアンダーパウダー、
　　　クミンシード、塩、ガラムマサラパ
　　　ウダー、ターメリックパウダーを同
　　　じ割合で調合

青唐辛子	1½本
バター	30g

油	適量
鶏モモ肉（一口大に切る）	400g
クミンシード	小さじ1
ニンニクとショウガのペースト	小さじ1

C

牛乳	1¼カップ
砂糖	大さじ4
ケチャップ	大さじ5
バター	30g

Ingredients（Serves 4）

50g cashew nuts
3 onions, sliced

A
2 tbsp olive oil
1 tsp whole cardamoms
1 tsp whole cloves
2 bay leaves
1 tsp whole black peppers
1 tsp cumin seeds
3 tbsp garlic and ginger paste*
　　*crush garlic and ginger separately and mix
　　　in equal proportions
1 tin (400g) whole tomatoes

B
1¼ cups warm milk
2 tbsp mixed spice*
　　*mixture of chilli powder, coriander
　　　powder, cumin seeds, salt, garam masala
　　　powder and turmeric powder in equal
　　　proportions
1½ green chillies
30g butter

Oil for stir-frying
400g chicken thigh, cut into bite-sized
　　pieces
1 tsp cumin seeds
1 tsp garlic and ginger paste

C
1¼ cups milk
4 tbsp sugar
5 tbsp ketchup
30g butter

From the cook

パキスタンでは、カレー
は薄いパンのようなチャ
パティと食べるのが定番
です。スパイスの香りを
引き立たせるために弱火
で調理していくことがお
いしく作るためのコツ。
レシピを紹介してくれた
難民の方は日本に来た
後、レストランで働きな
がら料理を学びました。

In Pakistan, this curry is
served with chapati, an
unleavened flatbread.
This dish should be
cooked on a low heat to
bring out the rich taste.
The refugee introduced
this recipe learned to
cook while working at a
restaurant after arriving
in Japan.

作り方

1. カシューナッツをやわらかくなるまで5分ほど茹で、水気を切り、冷ましておく。
2. 鍋に油をひき、タマネギとAを入れ、弱火でよく混ぜながら炒める。タマネギがしん　なりしたら強火にし、Bを加えて混ぜ、バターが溶けたら火からおろして冷ます。
3. 茹でておいたカシューナッツと2を一緒にミキサーにかけ、ペースト状にする。
4. フライパンに油をひき、鶏肉、クミンシード、ニンニク、ショウガのペーストを入れ、　鶏肉に火が通るまで焼く。
5. 別の鍋に少量の水を沸騰させ、3、4、Cを加え、バターが溶けるまで火にかけて味　をなじませる。

Directions

1. Boil the cashew nuts in water for 5 minutes to soften. Drain and cool.
2. Heat oil in a pot, add onions and A, and cook on a low heat while mixing well. When onions are translucent, change to a high heat. Add B and mix. Remove from the heat when the butter is melted. Cool.
3. Place boiled cashew nuts and the onion mixture into a mixer together and grind into a paste.
4. Heat oil and cook the chicken with cumin seed, garlic and ginger paste in a frying pan until the chicken is thoroughly cooked.
5. Boil a small amount of water in a pot. Add the cashew nuts mixture, chicken mixture, and C. Cook until the butter is melted and the flavours are blended.

Spicy Chicken
and Vegetable Stir-fry

鶏肉と野菜のスパイシー炒め

Sri Lanka

スリランカ

材料（4人分）

タマネギ（薄切り）	½個
赤唐辛子（輪切り）	1本
赤タマネギ（一口大に切る）	1個
トマト（一口大に切る）	1個
赤パプリカ（一口大に切る）	⅔個
チリパウダー	小さじ2
油	適量
鶏モモ肉（一口大に切る）	350g
塩	小さじ2
コショウ	小さじ1
チリソース	大さじ1⅓
レモン汁	小さじ2

Ingredients (Serves 4)

- ½ onion, sliced
- 1 red chilli, chopped
- 1 red onion, chopped
- 1 tomato, chopped
- ⅔ red pepper, chopped
- 2 tsp chilli powder
- Oil for frying/stir-frying
- 350g chicken thighs, cut into bite-sized pieces
- 2 tsp salt
- 1 tsp pepper
- 1⅓ tbsp chilli sauce
- 2 tsp lemon juice

From the cook

スリランカの料理は、スパイスをたっぷり使った味付けが特徴。各家庭には、代々伝わるスパイスの調合法があります。料理を作ってくれた難民の方は、母国に残って暮らす妻と電話する際に、調合について聞くこともあるそうです。スリランカでは、よく火の通った固めの肉が好まれるそうですが、お好みで鶏肉の揚げ時間を調整してください。

One of the characteristics of Sri Lankan cuisine is seasoning the ingredients with plenty of spices. Each family has its own special recipe for mixed spices. The refugee who taught this recipe sometimes calls his wife in Sri Lanka, to ask how to prepare their family blend. In Sri Lanka, "well done" is the preferred way to cook chicken. You can fry it to your liking.

作り方

1. フライパンに油をひき、タマネギが黄金色になるまで炒め、赤唐辛子、赤タマネギ、トマト、パプリカ、チリパウダーを加え、さらに炒める。
2. 鍋に油を熱し、鶏肉がきつね色になるまで揚げ、塩とコショウで味をつける。
3. 1のフライパンに鶏肉とチリソースを入れ、さっと炒めたら、火からおろす。
4. 最後にレモン汁を加えて混ぜ合わせる。

Directions

1. Heat oil in a frying pan and cook onion until golden. Add red chilli, red onion, tomato, red pepper and chilli powder. Continue to cook.
2. Fry chicken in oil until golden-brown. Season with salt and pepper.
3. Add the fried chicken and the chilli sauce to the onion mixture and stir. Remove from the heat.
4. Add lemon juice and mix.

Spiced Chicken and Potato Stew

鶏肉とジャガイモのスパイス煮込み

Burma

ビルマ

材料 （4人分）

鶏モモ肉	350g
塩、コショウ	少々
ターメリックパウダー	小さじ4
油	適量
タマネギ（みじん切り）	2個
ニンニク（みじん切り）	5かけ
ショウガ（みじん切り）	1かけ
A 松の実	小さじ1
ローリエの葉	3枚
シナモンスティック	1本
チリパウダー	小さじ1
水	2¼カップ
ジャガイモ（一口大に切る）	3個
ガラムマサラパウダー	小さじ2

Ingredients （Serves 4）

350g chicken thighs
Salt and pepper
4 tsp turmeric powder
Oil for stir-frying
2 onions, minced
5 garlic cloves, minced
1 piece ginger, minced

A | 1 tsp pine nuts
3 bay leaves
1 cinnamon stick
1 tsp chilli powder

2¼ cups water
3 potatoes, cut into bite-sized pieces
2 tsp garam masala powder

From the cook

ビルマ語では、「チェッタアールヒン」。「チェッタ」は鶏肉、「アール」はジャガイモ、「ヒン」は料理という意味です。ビルマ民族の料理には、ニンニクやショウガが多く使われます。ビルマ料理のレストラン情報はp.101をご覧ください。

In Myanmar (Burma), this stew is called *Kyetha Aloo Hin: kyetha* (chicken), *aloo* (potato) and *hin* (dish). Burmese food uses a lot of ginger and garlic. For Burmese restaurant information, please see page 101.

作り方

1. 鶏肉に塩、コショウ、ターメリックパウダー小さじ2をもみこみ、10〜15分ねかせたあと一口大に切る。
2. 鍋に油をひき、タマネギとターメリックパウダー小さじ2を炒める。タマネギがしんなりしたら、ニンニクとショウガを入れて香りを出し、鶏肉とAを加え、強火で炒める。
3. 水、ジャガイモ、ガラムマサラパウダー、コショウを加え、フタをして弱〜中火で煮込む。ジャガイモに火が通り、水分がなくなるまでさらに煮込む。

Directions

1. Rub chicken with salt, pepper, 2 tsp turmeric powder and leave for 10-15 minutes. Cut into bite-sized pieces.
2. Heat oil in a pot and cook onions with 2 tsp turmeric powder. When onions become translucent, add garlic and ginger. When aromatic, add chickens, A and cook on a high heat.
3. Add water, potatoes, garam masala powder and pepper. Cover and cook on a low–medium heat until potatoes are thoroughly cooked and almost no liquid remains in the pot.

Simple Chicken and Vegetable Curry

鶏肉と小松菜のカレー

Chin

チン

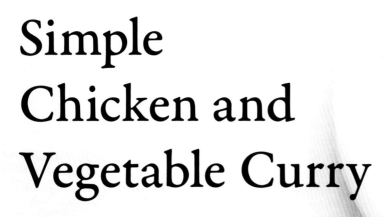

材料（4人分）

ニンニク（みじん切り）	2かけ
油	適量
タマネギ（一口大に切る）	1個
鶏モモ肉（一口大に切る）	350g
塩	適量
ターメリックパウダー	適量
七味唐辛子	適量
ジャガイモ（一口大に切る）	4個
水	4カップ
小松菜（ざく切り）	2束

※他の葉野菜でも代用可

Ingredients （Serves 4）

2 garlic cloves, minced

Oil for stir-frying

1 onion, cut into bite-sized pieces

350g chicken thigh, cut into bite-sized pieces

Salt

Turmeric powder

Shichimi (Japanese pepper)

4 potatoes, cut into bite-sized pieces

4 cups water

2 bunches komatsuna* (Japanese mustard spinach), coarsely chopped

*Or any leaf vegetable

From the cook

現地ではヤマイモの葉を乾燥させたものをスパイスとして入れることもあります。上の写真は、「ターンナーンファン」といい、チン民族の主食の一つです。アワ300gと豆1缶を混ぜ、蒸して作る主食で、炊飯器でも簡単に炊くことができます。水を少なめにすると、おいしく炊きあがります。

In Chin state, dried yam leaves are also added to this dish as a spice. Millet is one of their staple foods. You can make *Taang Ngan Huan* (as pictured above) by steaming 300g of millet and a tin of beans. You can also use a rice cooker, adding slightly less water as you would for cooking rice.

作り方

1. フライパンに油をひき、ニンニクを炒める。香りが出たら、タマネギ、鶏肉、塩、ターメリックパウダー、七味唐辛子を加え、よく炒める。
2. 鶏肉がきつね色になったら、ジャガイモを加えてよく炒め合わせ、水を入れ、フタをして煮込む。
3. ジャガイモに火が通ってきたら小松菜を入れ、しんなりしたら火を止める。

Directions

1. Heat oil in a frying pan with garlic. When aromatic, add onions, chicken, salt, turmeric powder, shichimi and cook well.
2. When the chicken is golden-brown, add the potatoes and mix well. Add water, cover and simmer until potatoes are thoroughly cooked.
3. Add komatsuna. Remove from the heat when the komatsuna has wilted.

Chicken Stew
Doro Wat

鶏肉の煮込み

ドロ・ワット

材料（4人分）

タマネギ（みじん切り）		3個
油		適量
A	ホールトマト（細かく刻む）	½缶（200g）
	ミックススパイス	大さじ4
	※ナツメグパウダー、黒コショウ、クローブ、シナモンパウダー、カイエンペッパー、パプリカパウダーをすりつぶし、同じ割合で調合	
	ニンニク（みじん切り）	3かけ
	ショウガ（みじん切り）	2かけ
	水	2½カップ
鶏肉（お好みの部位、一口大に切る）		350g
塩		少々
ミックススパイス		小さじ2
スパイスバター（作り方はp.60参照）		20g
ゆで卵		4個

Ingredients (Serves 4)

3 onions, minced		
Oil for stir-frying		
A	½ tin (200g) whole tomatoes, minced	
	4 tbsp mixed spice*	
	mixture of ground nutmeg, black pepper, cloves, cinnamon powder, cayenne pepper and paprika powder in equal proportions	
	3 garlic cloves, minced	
	2 pieces ginger, minced	
	2½ cups water	
350g chicken (any parts), cut into bite-sized pieces		
Salt		
2 tsp mixed spice		
20g spiced butter (refer to page 60)		
4 boiled eggs		

From the cook

アムハラ語で「ドロ」は鶏、「ワット」は煮込みの意味。エチオピアの主食であるインジェラを数枚重ね、その上に様々な料理をのせて盛り付けます。ドロ・ワットの油がインジェラに浸み込み、よく合います。食べる時は、何種類かの具材を右手でちぎったインジェラで、包んで食べます。家族が一つの大皿に手を伸ばして食べる風景は徐々に減ってきているようですが、エチオピアの家族団らんの場として大切にされてきました。

In Amharic, chicken is called *Doro*, stew is called *Wat*. Several pieces of *injera* (flatbread), which is a staple in Ethiopian cuisine, are layered to serve various dishes on top. The oil from *Doro Wat* soaks into the *injera* to create a great flavour. Tear pieces of *injera* with your right hand and wrap the *wat* and vegetables together when eating. Although dinner with the whole family who reach for food on one big plate is not seen as often anymore, it is still valued as a precious time for family bonding.

作り方

1. 鍋に油をひき、弱火でタマネギが色づくまで炒める。Aを加えてフタをし弱火でさらに30分ほど煮込む。
2. 別の鍋で、鶏肉を茹でる。
3. 1に、鶏肉、塩、ミックススパイス、スパイスバターを加え、フタをして弱火でさらに30分ほど煮込む。
4. ゆで卵に切り込みを入れて鍋に加え、よく絡める。野菜の炒めもの（p.58,59）などとインジェラ（p.61）とともに食べる。

Directions

1. In a large pot, heat oil on a low heat and cook the onions until deeply browned. Add A, cover and continue cooking for another 30 minutes.
2. In a separate pot, boil the chicken.
3. Add the boiled chicken, salt, mixed spice and spiced butter into the onion mixture. Cover and cook on a low heat for a further 30 minutes.
4. Make a few slits in the boiled eggs and add to the pot. Mix well with the stew. Serve with vegetable dishes such as (p.58, 59) and injera (p.61).

CHICKEN
SET
Doro Wat

From the cook

このレシピは手作りチーズを使用しています。料理を紹介してくれた難民の方が日本に来たばかりの頃、チーズを購入できる場所がわからず、仕方なく手作りに挑戦したとのこと。今では、いつも手作りをしているそうです。

This recipe uses home-made cheese. The refugee who shared this recipe did not know where to purchase cheese when she first arrived in Japan. So she decided to make it herself and now she only uses homemade cheese.

Vegetable and FreshCheese Stir-fry

青野菜とフレッシュチーズのソテー

Ethiopia

エチオピア

材料（4人分）

牛乳	5カップ
酢	大さじ3
小松菜（1cm幅に切る）	4束
※他の野菜でも代用可	
スパイスバター（作り方はp.60参照）	20g
カイエンペッパー	大さじ1

作り方

1. 鍋に牛乳と酢を入れてよく混ぜたら弱火にかける。白く分離してきたら（チーズの部分）、ざるで水気を切る。酢のにおいを取るため、ざるの中で水洗いし、再度水気を切る。
2. 小松菜は茹で、水気を切る。
3. フライパンでスパイスバターを熱し、小松菜を炒める。小松菜とバターがなじんだら、火からおろし、カイエンペッパーとチーズを加え、混ぜ合わせる。

Ingredients（Serves 4）

5 cups milk

3 tbsp vinegar

4 bunches komatsuna*, cut into 1cm-length pieces

*Or any leaf vegetable

20g spiced butter (refer to page 60)

1 tbsp cayenne pepper

Directions

1. Pour milk and vinegar into a pot and mix well before placing on a low heat. When the milk curdles, strain to separate the curds (cheese part). Rinse to remove the vinegar smell. Strain and put aside
2. Blanch komatsuna in boiling water. Drain.
3. In a frying pan, heat spiced butter and cook komatsuna on a medium heat. Remove from heat and mix with cayenne pepper and cheese.

From the cook

ドロ・ワットはイースターなどお祭りの時によく食べられる料理です。使用するスパイスの量や作り方は、民族ごとに異なり、その民族ならではの味が受け継がれています。

Doro Wat is often served during festivals such as Easter. Each ethnicity has a different mix of spices and methods of cooking. Their special flavours are passed down through generations.

Green Beans Stir-fry

インゲン豆と野菜の炒めもの

Ethiopia

エチオピア

材料（4人分）

ニンジン（5cmの棒状に切る）	1個
インゲン豆（スジを取り半分に切る）	300g
油	適量
タマネギ（薄切り）	1個
ニンニク（みじん切り）	2かけ
ショウガ（みじん切り）	2かけ
水	½カップ
塩、コショウ	少々

Ingredients（Serves 4）

1 carrot, cut into 5 cm-length sticks

300g green beans, remove strings and cut in half

Oil for frying/stir-frying

1 onion, sliced

2 garlic cloves, minced

2 pieces ginger, minced

½ cup water

Salt and pepper

作り方

1. 鍋に油を熱し、ニンジンとインゲン豆をそれぞれ1～2分カラッと揚げる。
2. フライパンに油を熱し、タマネギ、ニンニク、ショウガを炒める。タマネギに火が通ったら、ニンジン、インゲン豆、水を加え、さらに炒め、塩とコショウで味をととのえる。

Directions

1. Fry carrots and beans separately in oil for about 1-2 minutes.
2. In a frying pan, heat oil and cook the onion with garlic and ginger. When the onion is cooked, add carrots, beans, water, and cook. Flavour with salt and pepper.

From the cook

エチオピアではコサラツ
というセージに似た香り
のよいスパイスも入れま
す。生のものと粉末のも
の両方とも様々な料理に
使われています。

In Ethiopia, a spice called
koseret is also added. It
looks like sage, and both
fresh and powder
varieties are used in
Ethiopian cuisine.

Spiced Butter

スパイスバター

Ethiopia

エチオピア

Used in the *Doro Wat* and Green Vegetables and Fresh Cheese Stir-fry

ドロ・ワットや青野菜とチーズのソテーに使用

材料

A	クミンシード	小さじ1
	カルダモン（粒）	小さじ1
	アジョワンシード	小さじ1
無塩バター		200g

Ingredients

A	1 tsp cumin seeds
	1 tsp whole cardamom
	1 tsp ajowan seeds
200g unsalted butter	

作り方

1. Aをすり鉢で、すりつぶす。
2. 鍋に、Aとバターを入れ、弱火で熱する。
   バターが溶け、泡だってきたら、20
   〜30分熱して、火を止める。
3. バターをざるでこし、冷やして固める。

Directions

1. Mix and crush A in a mortar.
2. Place A and the butter into a pan and
   cook on a low heat. When the butter
   has melted and foam rises to the top,
   cook for a further 20-30 minutes.
   Turn off the heat.
3. Strain through a fine mesh sieve and
   cool until it solidifies.

Injera

インジェラ

Ethiopia
———
エチオピア

From the cook

本来は雑穀のテフを使用
していますが、日本では
手に入りにくいため、難
民の方々はそれぞれ独自
の方法で「故郷の味」を
再現しています。
ここで紹介するそば粉と
小麦粉を使ったものは、
「世界のレシピ集」
https://e-food.jp に
ご協力いただきました。

In Ethiopia, teff is used as
the main ingredient. As it
is difficult to find in
Japan, refugees often
think of their own ways
to recreate their "taste of
home".
The recipe using
buckwheat flour and flour
introduced here were
cooperated with "World
Recipe Collection"
https://e-food.jp.

材料（4人分）

そば粉	1カップ
小麦粉	½カップ
ドライイースト	小さじ1
ベーキングパウダー	小さじ¼
ヨーグルト	大さじ2
水	適量
油	適量

Ingredients（Serves 4）

1 cup buckwheat flour
½ cup flour
1 tsp dry yeast
¼ tsp baking powder
2 tbsp yoghurt
Water
Oil

作り方

1. ボウルでそば粉、小麦粉、ドライイー
   スト、ベーキングパウダー、ヨーグル
   トを混ぜ、ホットケーキのタネぐらい
   の固さになるまで水を加えて、よく混
   ぜる。
2. 濡れ布巾をかぶせて30分ほど寝かせ
   発酵させる。
3. フライパンに油をひき、クレープのよ
   うに薄く生地をのばし、片面だけ焼く。
   表面が泡立ち、固まってきたら火から
   おろす。

Directions

1. Mix the two flours, dry yeast, baking
   powder, yoghurt in a bowl and add
   water until it resembles a pancake
   dough.
2. Cover with a wet towel and put it aside
   for 30 minutes allowing it to ferment.
3. Heat oil in a frying pan and spread the
   dough like a thin pancake. Cooking
   only one side, remove from the heat
   when holes start to form on the
   surface and it is cooked through.

Fried Couscous Wrapped Meatballs

Icli Kofte

Kurd

クルド

挽き肉たっぷりクスクスの包み揚げ

イチリキョフテ

材料（4人分）

具

牛挽き肉		300g
塩		大さじ1
タマネギ（みじん切り）		1個
ニンニク（みじん切り）		1かけ
A	サルチャ（トマトペースト）	大さじ1½
	コショウ	大さじ1
	一味唐辛子	小さじ1
	チリパウダー	小さじ1
	サラダ油	大さじ5
	クルミ（みじん切り）	100g

クスクスの皮

B	クスクス	400g
	一味唐辛子	小さじ1
	コショウ	小さじ1
	チリパウダー	小さじ1
	塩	小さじ1½
	サルチャ（トマトペースト）	大さじ1½
	小麦粉	50g
湯		1カップ
油		適量

Ingredients （Serves 4）

For the filling

300g minced beef		
1 tbsp salt		
1 onion, minced		
1 garlic, minced		
A	1½ tbsp *salcasi* (tomato paste)	
	1 tbsp pepper	
	1 tsp red chilli flakes	
	1 tsp chilli powder	
	5 tbsp salad oil	
	100g walnuts, minced	

For the couscous mixture

B	400g couscous	
	1 tsp red chilli flakes	
	1 tsp pepper	
	1 tsp chilli powder	
	1½ tsp salt	
	1½ tbsp *salcasi* (tomato paste)	
	50g flour	
1 cup hot water		
Oil for stir-frying/frying		

From the cook

イチリキョフテは、生地を形にする作業に手間がかかり難しいですが、クルドではとても人気の料理です。生地をうまく作るコツは手の平に油と水をつけ、滑らせながら回していくこと。この料理を紹介してくれた難民の方は母親から代々伝わる生地の作り方を学びました。サルチャは、クルドの料理には欠かせないトマトペーストの調味料。日本では通販などで手に入れることができます。

Icli Kofte is a very popular dish for Kurdish people, although shaping the dough is time-consuming and requires a bit of practice. Put some water and oil on your palm to make shaping it easier. The refugee who contributed this recipe learnt it from her mother. *Salcasi* (tomato paste) is one of the vital ingredients for Kurdish cooking. It can be bought through mail order.

作り方

1. 鍋に油をひき、牛肉と塩を入れ中火で炒め、火が通ったらタマネギとニンニクを加えてさらに炒める。Aを入れてよく混ぜ合わせ、全体に火が通ったら、火からおろし冷ましておく。
2. ボウルにBを入れ、湯を少しずつ入れながら、パンをこねるように力強く混ぜ、耳たぶくらいの硬さになるまでよくこねる。
3. 手のひらに油と水をつけ、2をゴルフボールほどの大きさに丸め、真ん中に穴をあける。その中に1を大さじ2ほど入れて包み、口を閉じる。
4. 油でこんがりと揚げる。

Directions

1. Heat oil in a pan and cook minced beef with salt. When the beef is cooked, add onions and garlic and continue to cook. Add A and mix well. When cooked thoroughly, remove from heat to cool.
2. In a bowl, mix B. Add the hot water little by little, and knead as you would for bread.
3. Rub oil and water on your palms, and take a small piece of the couscous mixture and form into the size of a golf ball. With your fingers, make a whole in the middle. Place about 2 tbsp of the filling in the hole and wrap.
4. Fry until golden-brown.

Beef and Potato in Tomato Sauce

トマトソースの肉じゃが

Azeri

アゼリ

材料（4人分）

牛薄切り肉（一口大に切る）		240g
トマト（くし切り）		2個
ニンジン（一口大に切る）		½本
タマネギ（薄切り）		2個
ジャガイモ（一口大に切る）		4個
ニンニク（みじん切り）		5かけ
A	ターメリックパウダー	小さじ1
	黒コショウ	小さじ1
	ジンジャーパウダー	小さじ1
	白コショウ	少々
	カルダモンパウダー	少々
	シナモンパウダー	少々
	塩	少々
油		適量
B	トマトペースト	大さじ2
	酢	大さじ2
	レモン汁	大さじ2
	オリーブオイル	小さじ2
乾燥ミント		少々

Ingredients（Serves 4）

240g beef, thinly sliced and cut into
    bite-sized pieces

2 tomatoes, cut into wedges

½ carrot, cut into bite-sized pieces

2 onions, sliced

4 potatoes, cut into bite-sized pieces

5 garlic cloves, minced

A	1 tsp turmeric powder
	1 tsp black pepper
	1 tsp ginger powder
	Pinch of white pepper
	Pinch of cardamom powder
	Pinch of cinnamon powder
	Salt

Oil for stir-frying

B	2 tbsp tomato paste
	2 tbsp vinegar
	2 tbsp lemon juice
	2 tsp olive oil

Pinch of dried mint

From the cook

アゼリ地域では、本来は
ニンジンを入れません
が、甘みが出て日本人好
みの味になると、このレ
シピを紹介してくれた難
民の方がアレンジしてく
れました。この料理は冷
蔵庫で冷やしておき、食
べる直前に温めると、味
に深みが出てさらにおい
しく仕上がります。

In the Azeri region, this
recipe originally does not
include carrots; however,
the refugee who shared
this dish has added them
because he thinks that
Japanese people would
enjoy their sweetness. It
is also recommended to
cool the dish in the refrigerator and warm it up just
before serving for the
flavours to blend.

作り方

1. 鍋に油をひき、牛肉、トマト、ニンジン、タマネギ、ジャガイモ、ニンニク、Aを入れてよく炒め、フタをして10分ほど弱火にかける。
2. 野菜から十分に水分が出て、ジャガイモがやわらかくなったら、Bを加える。よく混ぜ、フタをして弱火で5〜7分蒸す。皿に盛り、乾燥ミントを散らす。

Directions

1. Cook beef, tomatoes, carrots, onions, potatoes, garlic and A in a pot with oil. Cover and cook on a low heat for 10 minutes.
2. When the vegetables begin to sweat and the potatoes are cooked, add B. Mix well, cover and steam on a low heat for another 5-7 minutes. Serve on a plate and sprinkle with dried mint.

Easy Home-cooked
Kebab

お家で簡単　フライパンケバブ

Azeri

アゼリ

材料（4人分）

タマネギ（すりおろす）	1個
牛挽き肉	350g
塩	少々
油	適量
トマト（くし切り）	2個
シシトウ	8本
青ジソの粉	少々

※青ジソのゆかりでも代用可

Ingredients（Serves 4）

1 onion, grated	
350g minced beef	
Salt	
Oil for stir-frying	
2 tomatoes, cut into wedges	
8 shishito peppers	
Pinch of shiso powder*	

*Or yukari powder

ケバブは中東とその周辺地域で食べられていますが、地域によって調理法が異なります。アゼリ風のケバブはあまり味付けせず、素材本来の味を楽しみます。パーティーなどの時は、今回のレシピのように形を整えますが、家族で食べる時は、フライパンにお肉を大きく広げて焼く方法がお手軽です（写真上）。最後に青ジソを散らしていますが、現地ではスマーグという調味料が使われています。

Kebab is a popular food in the Middle East and the surrounding areas, but seasoning and cooking methods vary depending on the regions. Azeri-style kebabs have less seasoning, allowing the natural taste of the ingredients to be enjoyed. Kebabs are shaped like this for special occasions such as parties, but the meat can be spread on a frying pan for family meals (as pictured above). A spice called *sumag* is used in the Azeri region, but it is replaced by shiso powder in this recipe.

作り方

1. すりおろしたタマネギ、牛肉、塩をボウルに入れ、手で十分にもみ、ラップをして冷蔵庫で10分冷やす。
2. 冷蔵庫から取り出し、肉から出た水分を切る。ラップの間に肉を広げ、手で肉を薄く伸ばす。
3. フライパンに油を熱し、成型した肉を入れ、片面がこんがり焼けてきたら裏返して焼く。
4. 肉を皿に移し、肉汁が出た同じフライパンでトマトとシシトウを軽く炒める。
5. 肉の上にトマトとシシトウをのせ、青ジソの粉を散らす。

Directions

1. Put grated onion, minced beef and a pinch of salt in a bowl and mix well. Cover and refrigerate for 10 minutes.
2. Remove the mixture from the refrigerator and drain any excess liquid. Spread the mixture between the sheets of plastic wrap, and make a thin patty.
3. Heat oil in a frying pan and place the meat patty in the pan. When the bottom is browned, flip the meat.
4. When done, remove the meat and place on a plate. Add the chopped tomatoes and shishito peppers to the pan with the meat juice and cook for a few minutes.
5. Place tomatoes and shishito peppers on the meat and sprinkle with shiso powder.

Ground Peanut and Beef Stew

ピーナッツと牛肉のシチュー

Cameroon
カメルーン

材料（4人分）

ピーナッツ		300g
水		4カップ
A	タマネギ	¼個
	パクチー	1½束
	セロリの葉	½束
	青ネギ	2cm
	シシトウ	4本
	トマト	3個
	ニンニク	4かけ
	ショウガ	4かけ
桜エビ		20g
油		適量
タマネギ（薄切り）		¼個
牛肉薄切り		250g
固形ブイヨン		1個
塩		少々

Ingredients（Serves 4）

300g peanuts		
4 cups water		
A	¼ onion	
	1½ bunches cilantro leaves	
	½ bunch celery leaves	
	2cm scallions	
	4 shishito peppers	
	3 tomatoes	
	4 garlic cloves	
	4 pieces ginger	
20g sakura shrimp		
Oil for stir-frying		
¼ onion, sliced		
250g beef, thinly sliced		
1 bouillon cube		
Salt		

From the cook

ピーナッツのシチューは
カメルーンの人気料理の
一つです。カメルーンで
は海で獲れる魚から牛や
羊まで幅広い食材が食べ
られています。同じ料理
の具材を肉と魚で取り替
えることも多く、今回使
用した牛肉の代わりに、
アジなどの魚を使うこと
もできます。ピーナッツ
の薄皮はフライパンで乾
煎りすると、めくれて簡
単にむくことができます。

This ground peanut stew is
a popular dish in Cameroon.
A wide variety of ingred-
ients, from sea fish to beef
and lamb are used. Meat
and fish are used inter-
changeably, so fish such as
horse mackerel can be
used in this dish. It is easy
to peel peanuts after dry
roasting them in a frying
pan for a couple of minutes.

作り方

1. ピーナッツは茶色の薄皮をむいて、ミキサーで細かく砕き、水3カップと合わせてお
く。
2. Aをミキサーにかけペースト状にする。
3. 桜エビをミキサーにかけ、細かくしておく。
4. 鍋に油をひき、タマネギと牛肉を炒める。火が通ったら、固形ブイヨン、塩、水1カ
ップを入れて煮込む。
5. 水と合わせたピーナッツ粉、ペースト状にしたA、桜エビを加えて、フタをして10分
火にかける。

Directions

1. Peel brown skin from the peanuts, grind in a mixer and mix with 3 cups water.
2. Put A in a mixer and blend into a paste.
3. Place the sakura shrimp in a mixer, and grind.
4. In a pot, heat the oil and cook the onion and beef. When cooked through, add a
bouillon cube, salt, 1 cup water and stew.
5. Add the ground peanuts paste, the paste of A and sakura shrimp. Cover and simmer
for about 10 minutes.

Peanut-seasoned Cabbage and Beef

キャベツと牛肉のピーナッツ和え

材料（4人分）

ピーナッツ	300g
水	2カップ
キャベツ（千切り）	1個
塩	少々
油	適量
タマネギ（薄切り）	½個
牛肉薄切り	300g
固形ブイヨン	2個

Ingredients（Serves 4）

- 300g peanuts
- 2 cups water
- 1 cabbage, shredded
- Salt
- Oil for stir-frying
- ½ onion, sliced
- 300g beef, thinly sliced
- 2 bouillon cubes

From the cook

カメルーンでは主食としてライスやトウモロコシの他に、プランティーンが食べられています。プランティーンとは調理用バナナで、日本で食べられているフルーツバナナよりも二回りほど大きく、生では食べず、茹でたり揚げたりします。この料理に限らず、カメルーンの料理全般に合わせられます。日本では通販や上野のアメ横などで手に入ります。

Besides rice and corn, plantains are eaten as a staple food in Cameroon. Plantains are known as cooking bananas and are twice as large as the bananas eaten in Japan. They are eaten boiled or fried. Plantains go well with any type of Cameroonian cuisine. You can buy plantains through mail order or at the Ameyoko market in Ueno.

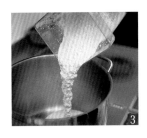

作り方

1. 鍋に茶色の薄皮をむいたピーナッツと水を入れ、やわらかくなるまで10分ほど茹でる。冷めたら、水ごとミキサーにかけ、ペースト状にする。
2. キャベツは塩茹でし、水気を切る。
3. 鍋に油をひき、タマネギと牛肉を炒める。ピーナッツペースト、茹でたキャベツ、固形ブイヨンを加えてよく混ぜ、フタをして全体に火が通り、味がなじむまで煮込む。

Directions

1. Peel skin from the peanuts and boil in 2 cups of water for about 10 minutes or until soft. When cooled, place in a mixer with the water and blend into a paste.
2. Boil the cabbage with salt. Drain.
3. Heat oil in a pot and cook the onion and beef. Add the peanut paste, cabbage, and bouillon cubes. Cover and stew until thoroughly cooked and flavoured.

Spicy Beef Stir-fry

牛挽き肉のスパイシー炒め

Kachin

カチン

From the cook

ミャンマー（ビルマ）の
少数民族は、それぞれ独
自の言葉を持っています。
この料理も、ミャンマー
の公用語であるビルマ語
では「アメーダーカチン
チェ」と呼ばれますが、
民族のカチン語では「シ
ャンカッ」と言います。

Ethnic minorities in
Myanmar (Burma) have
their own languages. This
dish is called *Amethar
Kachin Chet* in Burmese,
the official language of
Myanmar, but in their
native Kachin language,
it is called *Shan Hkak*.

材料（4人分）

A	牛挽き肉	350g
	ニンニク（みじん切り）	2かけ
	ショウガ（みじん切り）	1½かけ
	塩	小さじ1
	パクチー（細かく刻む）	⅓束
	赤唐辛子（細かく刻む） 2〜5本（お好みで）	
油		適量
水		大さじ1

Ingredients（Serves 4）

A	350g minced beef
	2 garlic cloves, minced
	1½ pieces ginger, minced
	1 tsp salt
	⅓ bunch cilantro leaves, minced
	2-5 red chillies (optional), minced
Oil for stir-frying	
1 tbsp water	

作り方

1. Aをボウルに入れ、手でよく混ぜる。
2. フライパンに油をひき、1を入れ、強火で1分ほどパラパラになるよう炒めたら、水を加えフタをし、2分ほど蒸し焼きにする。

Directions

1. Place A in a bowl and mix well by hand.
2. Heat oil in a frying pan and add the meat mixture. Cook on a high heat for 1 minute until it becomes crumbly. Add 1 tbsp water and cover for another 2 minutes.

Beef and Green Banana Tomato Stew

牛肉とグリーンバナナのトマト煮込み

材料（4人分）

牛肉（一口大に切る）	300g
水	3カップ
サラダ油	大さじ1
トマト（くし切り）	1個
ホールトマト	½缶（200g）
タマネギ（薄切り）	½個
塩	適量
カレーパウダー	小さじ1
グリーンバナナ（皮をむいて一口大に切る）	4本

※プランティーン（2本）、サツマイモ（4本）
でも代用可

Ingredients（Serves 4）

300g beef, cut into bite-sized pieces

3 cups water

1 tbsp salad oil

1 tomato, cut into wedges

½ tin (200g) whole tomatoes

½ onion, sliced

Salt

1 tsp curry powder

4 green bananas*, peeled and cut into
bite-sized pieces

*or 2 plantains or 4 sweet potatoes

From the cook

日本ではアフリカ産のグ
リーンバナナを手に入れ
ることは難しいですが、
フィリピン産の調理用バ
ナナで代用できます。太
くて短いフィリピン産の
ものがウガンダの味とよ
く似ており、通販や上野
のアメ横などで手に入れ
ることができます。昼食
や夕食ではグリーンバナ
ナを蒸してつぶしたもの
を主食として食べますが、
朝食では、手軽に一緒に
煮込んでいただくのが定
番です。

In this recipe, green
bananas from the Philip-
pines can be used instead
of Ugandan green bananas
as they are not as popular
in Japan. Philippine cooking
bananas, which are thicker
and shorter, have a similar
taste to those from Uganda.
They can be bought through
mail order or in the
Ameyoko market in Ueno.
Mashed green bananas are
served as a staple food for
lunch and dinner. This
easily cooked version is
usually served for break-
fast.

作り方

1. 鍋に牛肉を入れ、水1½カップを加えて茹でる。水がなくなったら、サラダ油を加え
て炒める。
2. トマト、ホールトマト、タマネギ、塩、カレーパウダーを加える。タマネギがしんな
りしてきたら、水1½カップとグリーンバナナを加え、よく混ぜ、グリーンバナナが
やわらかくなるまで煮る。

Directions

1. Place beef and 1½ cups water in a pot and boil. When almost no liquid remains in the
pot, add salad oil and cook.
2. Add tomato, whole tomatoes, onions, salt and curry powder. When onions are translucent, add 1½ cups water and green bananas. Mix well and cook until the green bananas are thoroughly cooked.

Stuffed Vegetable
Dolma

ピーマンとナスの肉詰め煮込み

ドルマ

材料（4人分）

A	米	1½カップ
	牛挽き肉	100g
	ニンニク（みじん切り）	4かけ
	タマネギ（みじん切り）	½個
	コショウ	小さじ1
	チリパウダー	小さじ1
	レモン汁	大さじ1½
	サラダ油	大さじ3
	一味唐辛子	少々
ナス		8個
ピーマン		8個
B	レモン汁	大さじ2
	サルチャ（トマトペースト）	小さじ1½
	塩	少々
	サラダ油	大さじ2
	水	1½カップ

Ingredients（Serves 4）

A	1½ cups uncooked rice	
	100g minced beef	
	4 garlic cloves, minced	
	½ onion, minced	
	1 tsp pepper	
	1 tsp chilli powder	
	1½ tbsp lemon juice	
	3 tbsp salad oil	
	Pinch of red chilli flakes	
8 aubergines		
8 green peppers		
B	2 tbsp lemon juice	
	1½ tsp *salsica* (tomato paste)	
	Salt	
	2 tbsp salad oil	
	1½ cups water	

From the cook

ドルマとは「詰められたもの」という意味で、旬の様々な野菜が使われ、ブドウの葉、かぼちゃ、パプリカ、ズッキーニ、トマトなど、季節によって色鮮やかな野菜が食卓に並びます。野菜の中に具材を詰めすぎるとお米が膨らみ破裂する恐れがあるので要注意です。

Dolma means "stuffed" and Kurdish cooking uses various types of seasonal vegetables such as grape leaves, pumpkins, peppers, courgettes and tomatoes, adding colour to the table. It is best when you leave some space when stuffing the vegetables so that the rice has room to expand when cooked.

作り方

1. Aをボウルでよく混ぜる。
2. ナスとピーマンはヘタを取る（ヘタも使うので捨てないでおく）。ナスはペティナイフかスプーンなどで中をくり抜き、ピーマンは種を取る。
3. ナスとピーマンを3分ほど茹でる。
4. 茹でたナスとピーマンの中に、Aを⅔程度まで入れ、ヘタでフタをする。
5. 具を詰めたナスとピーマンを鍋に入れ、合わせておいたBを加え、落しブタをして弱火で35分ほど煮る。

Directions

1. Mix A in a bowl.
2. Cut the stems off the aubergines and green peppers. (Do not throw them away as the stems will be used later.) Remove the seeds of the aubergines with a paring knife or spoon. Remove the seeds from the green peppers.
3. Blanch aubergines and green peppers for 3 minutes.
4. Spoon mixture A in the aubergines and green peppers until ⅔ full. Cover vegetables with the stem.
5. In a pot, place stuffed aubergines and green peppers. Mix B together and add to the pot. Cook on a low heat for 35 minutes with a drop lid.

Burmese-style Noodles with Kinako

きな粉入りビルマ風サラダうどん

材料（4人分）

鶏モモ肉（角切り）		200g
A	砂糖	小さじ1
	ターメリックパウダー	小さじ1
	ナンプラー	小さじ1
油		適量
タマネギ（みじん切り）		1個
ターメリックパウダー		大さじ2
ニンニク（すりおろす）		3かけ
ショウガ（すりおろす）		1かけ
チリパウダー		小さじ1
B	塩、コショウ	少々
	ナンプラー	大さじ2
	水	½カップ
うどん		4玉
キャベツ（千切り）		⅛個
タマネギ（薄切り）		½個
レモン汁		大さじ1
ナンプラー（仕上げ用）		小さじ1
きな粉		大さじ1⅓
一味唐辛子		小さじ1
塩		少々
パクチー		少々
※青ネギなどでも代用可		
ゆで卵（半分に切る）		2個

Ingredients（Serves 4）

200g chicken thigh, diced		
A	1 tsp sugar	
	1 tsp turmeric powder	
	1 tsp fish sauce, or soy sauce	
Oil for stir-frying		
1 onion, minced		
2 tbsp turmeric powder		
3 garlic cloves, grated		
1 piece ginger, grated		
1 tsp chilli powder		
B	Salt and pepper	
	2 tbsp fish sauce, or soy sauce	
	½ cup water	
4 packs (800g) udon noodles		
⅛ cabbage, shredded		
½ onion, sliced		
1 tbsp lemon juice		
1 tsp fish sauce, or soy sauce (to finish)		
1⅓ tbsp kinako powder (soybean flour)		
1 tsp chilli flakes		
Salt		
Fresh cilantro leaves*, chopped		
*Or spring onion		
2 boiled eggs, cut into half		

From the cook

ビルマでは、ひよこ豆の粉を使いますが、今回はきな粉で代用しました。ビルマでひよこ豆の粉は、麺料理だけでなく、スープ、サラダなどにも使う、定番材料の一つです。ビルマ料理では、生の粉と炒った粉の二種類のひよこ豆の粉を使い分けています。高田馬場は、リトルヤンゴンと呼ばれており、ビルマ料理レストランがたくさんあります。ビルマ民族の料理は難民の方が経営するレストラン「ルビー」にご協力いただきました。ビルマ料理レストラン情報は、p.101をご覧ください。

In this dish, Kinako powder (soybean flour) is used as a substitute for garbanzo flour which is used in Burma. Garbanzo flour is a staple ingredients often used for such dishes as noodle, soup, salad and so on. In Burmese cuisine, two kinds of garbanzo flour, roasted and raw, are used. Takadanobaba is known as little Yangon, and there are many Burmese restaurants. Burmese dishes were provided by the restaurant, Ruby, run by a refugee. For information on Burmese restaurant, please see page 101.

作り方

1. 鶏肉にAをもみこんでおく。
2. フライパンに油をひき、みじん切りしたタマネギ、ターメリックパウダーを入れ火が通るまで炒める。ショウガ、ニンニク、チリパウダーを加え、香りが出るまでさらに炒める。
3. 鶏肉とBを加えて焦げないように炒める。
4. 別の鍋でうどんを茹で、水気を切り、ボウルに入れておく。
5. うどんの上にキャベツ、薄切りにしたタマネギ、鶏肉をのせ、レモン汁、ナンプラー、きな粉、一味唐辛子、塩をかけ、全体をよく和える。
6. 仕上げにパクチーと半分に切ったゆで卵を飾りつける。

Directions

1. Rub chickens with A.
2. Heat oil in a frying pan, add the minced onion and turmeric powder and stir until thoroughly cooked. Add garlic, ginger and chilli powder and cook until it is aromatic.
3. Add chicken and B to the frying pan and stir, making sure not to burn them.
4. Boil udon in a separate pot. Drain and put in a bowl.
5. Add cabbage, sliced onions, chicken, lemon juice, fish sauce, kinako powder, chilli flakes and salt to the udon and mix well.
6. Garnish with fresh cilantro leaves and half-cut boiled eggs.

Pakistani *Biryani*

パキスタン風炊き込みごはん　ビリヤニ

材料 (4人分)

A	カルダモン (緑色)	4粒
	クローブ	6粒
	ローリエの葉	2枚
	シナモンスティック	2本
	黒コショウ	10粒
油		適量
タマネギ (薄切り)		1½個
カシューナッツ		20g
青唐辛子 (輪切り)		1½本
カットトマト		1缶 (400g)
ニンニクとショウガのペースト		大さじ3

※ニンニクとショウガをそれぞれすりつぶし、
同じ割合で混ぜ合わせる

| ミックススパイス | 大さじ2 |

※チリパウダー、コリアンダーパウダー、ク
ミンシード、塩、ガラムマサラパウダー、
ターメリックパウダーを同じ割合で調合

水	3カップ
鶏肉 (一口大に切る)	300g
バター	40g
塩	少々
バスマティライス	2カップ

Ingredients (Serves 4)

A	4 whole green cardamoms
	6 whole cloves
	2 bay leaves
	2 cinnamon sticks
	10 whole black peppers
Oil for stir-frying	
1½ onion, sliced	
20g cashew nuts	
1½ green chillies, chopped	
1 tin (400g) cut tomatoes	
3 tbsp garlic and ginger paste*	

*crush garlic and ginger separately and mix in
equal proportions

2 tbsp mixed spice*

*mixture of chilli powder, coriander powder,
cumin seeds, salt, garam masala powder, turmeric powder in equal proportions

3 cups water
300g chicken, cut into bite-sized pieces
40g butter
Salt
2 cups basmati rice

From the cook

ビリヤニは、米と具材を
混ぜた炊き込みご飯で、
パキスタンでは結婚式な
どのお祝い事などで食さ
れます。鶏肉以外にもラ
ム肉や野菜を使った様々
な種類のものがあるとい
います。本来は鶏肉やミ
ントの葉などの具材を混
ぜた何種類かのご飯を作
り、層を重ねていくとい
う、非常に複雑で時間の
かかる料理。家庭料理と
いうよりはプロのシェフ
が作るものという位置づ
けなのですが、今回は家
庭でも気軽に作れるよう
にこのレシピを紹介して
くれた難民の方がアレン
ジしてくれました。

Biryani is traditionally
served at gatherings like
weddings or other
celebrations. Chicken
can be substituted with
lamb or vegetables. The
dish is originally cooked
in a rather complicated
way and is layered with
several types of rice with
ingredients such as
chicken and mint leaves.
Usually prepared by
professional chefs, this
refugee has produced a
recipe that can be
prepared easily at home.

作り方

1. 鍋に油をひき、Aを1〜2分炒める。タマネギ、カシューナッツ、青唐辛子、カット
トマト、ニンニクとショウガのペースト、ミックススパイス、水1カップを入れ、タ
マネギに火が通るまで煮る。
2. 鶏肉、バター、塩を加え、フタをして弱火にかけ、焦げつかないよう混ぜながら煮る。
3. 水2カップを加え、沸騰してきたらバスマティライスを加える。最初は中火で、米が
半透明になったら弱火にしてフタをする。そのまま水がなくなるまで火にかける。

Directions

1. Heat oil in a pot, add A and cook for 1-2 minutes. Add onions, cashew nuts, green
chillies, cut tomatoes, garlic and ginger paste and mixed spice. Add 1 cup water and
boil until the onions are cooked.
2. Add chicken, butter and salt. Cover and cook on a low heat, stirring occasionally.
3. Add 2 cups water to the pot and bring to the boil, add basmati rice. Cook on a medium heat at first. When the rice becomes translucent, cover and cook on a low heat
until no liquid remains.

Chicken and
Pomegranate Rice

鶏肉とザクロのカラフルライス

Iran

イラン

材料（4人分）

乾燥ザクロ	小さじ4
バター（ザクロ用）	5g
（ライス用）	20g
（鶏肉用）	10g
ペルシャライス／ バスマティライス	2カップ
水	2½カップ
塩	小さじ2
鶏モモ肉（一口大に切る）	300g
タマネギ（薄切り）	½個
サフラン	小さじ2

Ingredients（Serves 4）

4 tsp dried pomegranates	
Butter	5g for pomegranates
	20g for rice
	10g for chicken
2 cups Persian or basmati rice	
2½ cups water	
2 tsp salt	
300g chicken thigh, cut into bite-sized pieces	
½ onion, sliced	
2 tsp Saffron	

From the cook

「ゼレシュク　ポロ」と呼ばれる、イランではおなじみの、パーティーに欠かせない人気料理です。この料理のポイントは乾燥ザクロ（写真上）の赤い色とサフランライスの黄色の彩り。難民の方曰く、味のアクセントとなる乾燥ザクロの酸味は日本の梅干しと少し似ているためか、日本人の知り合いにとても好評だったとのこと。乾燥ザクロは、通販などで手に入れることができます。

This is called *Zereshk Polo* and is one of the most popular dishes served at parties in Iran. The colour comes from dried pomegranate (red) and saffron (yellow). The combination of these two make the rice colourful and tasty. This recipe is popular among Japanese friends of the refugee as the sour taste of the dried pomegranate is similar to the taste of umeboshi (sour plum).Dried pomegranates, as pictured above, can be bought through mail order.

作り方

1. 乾燥ザクロは水につけてもどし、フライパンでバターと軽く炒める。
2. 鍋にペルシャライス、水2カップ、バター、塩小さじ1を入れて炊く。
3. 別の鍋に鶏肉、タマネギ、塩小さじ1を入れ、アクを取りながら20分ほど、鶏肉がやわらかくなるまで茹でる。鶏肉はざるにあげ、タマネギは捨てる。
4. フライパンにバターを熱し、鶏肉とサフラン小さじ1を入れ、香りをつけながら焼く。
5. 炊き上がったペルシャライスを¼ほどをとり、水½カップで溶いたサフラン小さじ1と混ぜ、黄色のサフランライスを作る。
6. 白いままのペルシャライスを皿に平らに盛る。その上に二層になるようにサフランで色づけしたライスを盛る。ライスの上に鶏肉をのせ、ザクロを散らす。

Directions

1. Soak pomegranates in water. Melt butter in a pan and cook the pomegranate.
2. Cook the Persian rice with 2 cups water, butter and 1 tsp salt.
3. In a separate pot, boil the chicken, onions and 1 tsp salt. Cook for 20 minutes until the chicken becomes tender, skimming off any foam that forms. Drain and discard the onions.
4. Melt the butter in a frying pan and add the chicken and 1 tsp saffron.
5. Place about ¼ of the cooked rice in a bowl. Dissolve 1 tsp saffron with ½ cup water and add the rice to absorb the colour.
6. Place the remaining white rice on a serving plate. Layer the coloured saffron rice on top. Top with chicken and pomegranates.

Corn Stew

トウモロコシの煮込み

Chin
———
チン

材料（4人分）		Ingredients（Serves 4）	
乾燥トウモロコシ	400g	400g dried sweet corn	

野菜版－ヴァイミンチン

		Vegetable version, Vaimiin ciim	
インゲン豆	300g	300g green beans	
小松菜（ざく切り）	1束	1 bunch komatsuna* (Japanese mustard spinach), cut coarsely	
※他の葉野菜でも代用可		*Or any leaf vegetable*	

牛肉版－サブティ

		Beef version, Sa Buti	
牛モツ	200g	200g beef giblets	
牛こま切れ肉	200g	200g beef, thinly sliced	

From the cook

トウモロコシやアワを主食とするチン民族ならではの一品。調味料での味付けはしていないため、スパイシーサラダ（p.10）を入れて食べます。加える具材によって名前が異なり、野菜入りを「ヴァイミンチン」、肉入りを「サブティ」と呼びます。上の写真は、ひょうたんで作ったチンの伝統的なスプーン。ひょうたんは食材としても使われ、カレーに入れるジャガイモの代わりにもなるそうです。乾燥トウモロコシはアジア・中華食材店などで購入できます。

This recipe is a typical Chin dish that uses corn and millet as a staple food. It is served with the spicy salad (p.10) as the dish is not seasoned. Names depend on the ingredients. By adding vegetables, it is called *Vaimiin Ciim* and with meat it is called *Sa Buti*. The spoon shown in the picture above is made from the gourd fruit. Gourd is also used in Chin cooking and is a great substitute for potatoes used in Chin curry. Dried sweet corn can be bought at Asian or Chinese food shops.

作り方　野菜版－ヴァイミンチン

1. 乾燥トウモロコシを蒸し器で20分蒸す。
2. 鍋に、蒸したトウモロコシ、インゲン豆、小松菜を加え、具が浸るぐらいまで水を入れ、やわらかくなるまで茹でる。

作り方　牛肉版－サブティ

1. 乾燥トウモロコシを蒸し器で20分蒸す。
2. 鍋に牛モツを入れ、浸るぐらいまで水を加え、やわらかくなるまで煮たら、牛こま切れ肉を入れて煮込む。
3. 蒸した乾燥トウモロコシを加え、ひと煮たちさせる。

Directions for Vegetable version, *Vaimin ciim*

1. Steam dried corn for 20 minutes.
2. Add steamed corn, green beans, komatsuna and enough water to cover. Cook until they are soft.

Directions for Beef version, *Sa Buti*

1. Steam dried corn for 20 minutes.
2. Simmer the beef giblets in a pot with enough water to cover them. Once they are cooked, add the sliced beef and cook well.
3. Add the steamed corn to the pot and cook until they are soft.

Yellow Rice Pudding

イエローライスの冷たいデザート

Iran

イラン

材料（4人分）

ペルシャライス	⅔カップ
水	4カップ
砂糖（40gづつ3回使用）	120g
サフラン	小さじ½
ピスタチオ（みじん切り）	40g
ローズウォーター（香り付け用）	¼カップ
シナモンパウダー（飾り付け用）	適量
アーモンド、ピスタチオ（飾り付け用）	適量

Ingredients（Serves 4）

- ⅔ cup Persian rice
- 4 cups water
- 120g sugar (divided into 3 portions)
- ½ tsp saffron
- 40g pistachios, finely chopped
- ¼ cup rosewater (for fragrance)
- Cinnamon powder (to garnish)
- Almonds, pistachios (to garnish)

作り方

1. 鍋にペルシャライス、水、砂糖40gを加えて火にかける。沸騰したら砂糖40gを加え、ペルシャライスの形がなくなるまで煮る。
2. サフラン、ピスタチオ、ローズウォーター、残りの砂糖40gを加え、さらに水分がなくなったら、火を止め大皿に平たく盛る。
3. 飾りつけ用のアーモンドとピスタチオを5分ほど茹で、水気を切り、細かく刻んでおく。盛りつけたペルシャライスの上にシナモン、アーモンド、ピスタチオで飾りつけ、冷蔵庫でよく冷やす。

Directions

1. Place the Persian rice with water and 40g sugar in a pot and bring to the boil. Add another 40g sugar and cook until the rice becomes mushy.
2. Add saffron, chopped pistachios, rosewater and the remaining 40g of sugar. Continue cooking to reduce the liquid. Pour into a large bowl.
3. Blanch almonds and pistachios for 5 minutes. Drain and chop finely. Decorate the Persian rice by sprinkling the cinnamon, almonds and pistachios on top. Refrigerate and serve cool.

From the cook

「ショレザルド」と呼ばれる、イランでとても人気のデザートです。ポイントは砂糖をたっぷり加えること、サフランとローズウォーターのバランスに気を付けること、食べる前によく冷やすことの3点です。シナモンやピスタチオ、ナッツのデコレーションが、見た目にも楽しいデザートです。難民の方は、子どもの頃に母親が作ってくれたショレザルドの作り方を覚えており、日本でも時々作っては、同じイラン出身の友人や、日本人の友人に振舞うそうです。サフランやローズウォーターは通販、上野のアメ横などで購入できます。

This is called *Sholeh Zard* and is a popular dessert in Iran. Important tips are to add plenty of sugar, a balanced usage of saffron and rosewater, and to refrigerate well before serving. This dessert is also pleasing to the eye as people enjoy decorating it with cinnamon, pistachios and other nuts. The refugee who provided this recipe remembers how his mother cooked for him as a child. He now serves it to his Iranian and Japanese friends. Saffron and rosewater can be bought through mail order or in the Ameyoko market in Ueno.

Bread Pudding with Nuts and Raisins

ナッツとレーズンのパンプティング

Pakistan

パキスタン

From the cook

このデザートは来客をもてなす時や、ラマダン、結婚式、卒業式など特別なパーティーで食べられています。レーズンやカシューナッツ以外のドライフルーツ、ナッツを使ってもおいしくいただけます。

This dessert is served on special occasions such as entertaining guests, Ramadan, weddings and graduation ceremonies. Raisins and cashew nuts can be substituted with other dried fruits and nuts.

材料 （4人分）

砂糖	80g
卵	4個
牛乳	¾カップ
バター	100g
食パン（8枚切りをサイコロ状に切る）	8枚
カシューナッツ	70g
レーズン	10g

Ingredients （Serves 4）

- 80g sugar
- 4 eggs
- ¾ cup milk
- 100g butter
- 8 slices bread, diced
- 70g cashew nuts
- 10g raisins

作り方

1. 砂糖、卵、牛乳を混ぜ合わせる。
2. 鍋にバターを溶かし、切った食パンと1を加え、弱火にかけながら混ぜる。
3. パンが充分に水分を吸ったら、カシューナッツとレーズンを入れ、さらによく混ぜる。
   ※温冷ともにおいしく召し上がれます。

Directions

1. Mix sugar, eggs and milk well.
2. Melt the butter in a pot. Add the cut bread and the egg mixture. Stir over a low heat.
3. When the bread has absorbed the liquid, add the cashew nuts and raisins. Mix well.
   *serve warm or cold

Tapioca Milk with Sweet Potatoes

タピオカとサツマイモのデザート

Burma

ビルマ

From the cook

現地では牛乳ではなくコ
コナッツミルクを使いま
す。ビルマ民族の料理で
は、タピオカミルクにイ
モを入れて食べるのが習
慣となっています。
ビルマ料理レストラン情
報は、p.101をご覧くだ
さい。

In Myanmar (Burma),
coconut milk is used
instead of milk. In
Burmese cuisine, it is a
custom to add potatoes
to the tapioca. For
information on Burmese
restaurant, please see
page 101.

材料（4人分）

タピオカ	100g
サツマイモ（1cm角に切る）	1本
牛乳（もしくはココナッツミルク）	2½カップ
砂糖	大さじ2
塩	少々

Ingredients（Serves 4）

100g tapioca
1 sweet potato, 1cm diced
2½ cups milk or coconut milk
2 tbsp sugar
Salt

作り方

1. 白い芯がなくなるまでタピオカを茹で、水で洗う。
2. サツマイモを茹で、水気を切っておく。
3. 鍋に牛乳、砂糖、塩を入れ、混ぜながら火にかける。
4. 沸騰する直前に火を止め、タピオカとサツマイモを加えて混ぜる。
   ※温冷ともにおいしく召し上がれます。

Directions

1. Boil the tapioca until soft. Rinse in water.
2. Boil sweet potatoes and drain.
3. Place milk, sugar and salt in a pot and cook while stirring.
4. Turn off the heat just before it starts to boil. Add the tapioca and sweet potato and mix.
   *serve warm or cold

Karen's Rice Dumplings in Coconut Milk

カレンのココナッツミルク白玉

Karen

カレン

From the cook

カレン語では「おもちの実」という意味合いをもつデザート。丸く型どったおもちが果実の実に似ていることが由来だそう。写真にうつっているのは、難民の方が持ってきた、民族衣装を着た人形です。難民の方も、撮影の時には手作りの民族衣装を着て来てくれました。

This dessert is called "fruit of rice dumpling" in the Karen language, as the ball-shaped rice dumplings resemble one of their native fruits. The dolls wearing traditional costume (pictured) were brought in by the refugee who provided this recipe. On the day of the photo shoot, the refugee wore his handmade traditional costume.

材料 (4人分)

だんご粉（または白玉粉）	200g
水	¾カップ
ココナッツミルク	¾カップ
砂糖	大さじ3
塩	少々
ココナッツチップ（飾り付け用）	少々

Ingredients (Serves 4)

200g dango (or shiratama) powder	
¾ cups water	
¾ cups coconut milk	
3 tbsp sugar	
Salt	
Coconut flakes (to garnish)	

作り方

1. だんごの粉（または白玉粉）に水を加えてこね、やわらかくなったら一口サイズに丸め、沸騰した湯に入れ、浮いてきたらそのまま1分茹でる。
2. 鍋にココナッツミルクを入れて温め、砂糖と塩を入れる。
3. だんごを器にうつし、2をかけ、ココナッツチップを散らす。

Directions

1. Add water to the dango powder and knead until the dough becomes soft. Make bite-sized balls and cook in boiling water. When the dumplings start to float, cook for another minute.
2. Pour coconut milk into a pot and heat. Add sugar and salt.
3. Place dumplings in a bowl and pour the coconut milk mixture onto the balls. Sprinkle with coconut chips.

地図、民族情報

アゼリ
アゼルバイジャンやイランの北西部に暮らしている民族。肥沃な大地からとれるハーブやスパイスを使った料理が特徴です。

p.12, 20, 64, 66

クルド
トルコ、イラン、イラク、シリア等の国境地帯に暮らしている民族で、「国を持たない世界最大の民族」と呼ばれています。山岳地帯ですが、肥沃な土地で、ぶどうなどの果実やクルミなどの作物が栽培されています。

p.16, 18, 19, 62, 76

カメルーン
「アフリカの縮図」とも称されるほど、地域によって気候が異なり、料理もバラエティ豊か。英語圏とフランス語圏に分かれた対立が続いています。

p.36, 68, 70

イラン
公用語はペルシャ語で、国教はシーア派イスラム教。ザクロやバラなどを使った独自の料理があります。表現や集会の自由、信教の自由が厳しく制限されています。

p.46, 82, 86

コンゴ民主共和国
国土の中央を流れるコンゴ川や湖で魚が豊富にとれ、食されています。イモ類やトウモロコシなど穀物の種類も多様。周辺国の影響を受けた紛争を抱え、2019年の政権移行後も国内では暴力行為から逃れる人が続いています。

p.30, 32

ウガンダ
赤道直下の熱帯地域で、バナナやトウモロコシの粉などが主食として食べられています。性的マイノリティや政治活動家の自由が厳しく制限されています。

p.28, 74

エチオピア
公用語はアムハラ語。高地に位置し、クレープのようなパン「インジェラ」に「ワット」と呼ばれる煮込み料理を組み合わせる食べ方が特徴です。民族間での対立や自由な政治活動への妨げにより、社会的な混乱が起きてきました。現在も多数の死者を出す暴動が起こるなど、不安定な状況があります。

p.56, 58, 59, 60, 61

Azeri

Kurd

Iran

Cameroon

Ethiopia

Uganda

D.R. Congo

パキスタン

60以上の言語が話されているといわれるほど多様性に富み、料理も種類が豊富。国教はイスラム教ですが、異なる宗派や民族、政党間の対立が続いています。

p.48, 80, 88

ネパール

多民族・多言語国家ですが、カレーやご飯、漬物などを組み合わせて食べるスタイルは共通しています。王政による圧政から解放された後の、政治的な混乱から逃れた方が多くいます。

p.14, 24, 42

バングラデシュ

ガンジス川をはじめ、水資源が豊富で、魚がよく食べられています。コメの消費量は世界有数。政党間や民族間、宗教間の対立が、社会的な混乱を引き起こしています。

p.26, 34

Pakistan

Nepal

Bangladesh

Myanmar/
Burma

Sri Lanka

ミャンマー（ビルマ）

ビルマ民族と様々な少数民族から成り立っています。長期にわたる軍事政権の下、民主活動家や少数民族への迫害で、多くの人が国を離れました。近年では特に、ロヒンギャへの迫害と難民の流出が世界の注目を集めています。

ビルマ

ミャンマー（ビルマ）人口の約70%を占めています。多くの人が仏教を信仰しています。　　　　p.52, 78, 90

カチン

中国とインドに国境を接する山間地域に住んでおり、料理の味付けも両国の影響を受けています。大多数はキリスト教を信仰しています。　　p.44, 72

カレン

ミャンマー（ビルマ）の人口の約7%を占めるのがカレン民族。チベットを源流としたサルウィン川が流れ、川魚がよく食べられています。

p.38, 40, 92

チン

チン民族は標高3,000mの高山地域に住み、伝統的にはアワやトウモロコシが食べられてきました。大多数はキリスト教を信仰しています。

p.10, 54, 84

スリランカ

インド洋に浮かぶ島国で、貿易や周辺国の影響を受けながら、様々なスパイスを使う、独自の料理を生みだしました。人口の70%を占めるシンハラ民族と少数派のタミル民族間の紛争や政治的な混乱により、多くの人が故郷を追われました。

p.22, 50

備考：
難民となる理由は人によって様々で、本書にレシピを提供してくださった難民の方が、必ずしも上記の理由で逃れてきたわけありません。ここで記載している各国・地域の情報は一部に過ぎず、政治社会情勢も日々変化していることをご了承ください。

Map and Ethnic Information

Azeri

The Azeri are an ethnic group that live in the Republic of Azerbaijan and the northeast of Iran. Its cuisine is unique for its use of the herbs and spices that are harvested from the country's rich soil. p.12, 20, 64, 66

Azeri

Kurd

The Kurdish people live in the border region of Turkey, Iran, Iraq, and Syria and are known as the largest ethnicity in the world without a country of its own. Although it is a mountainous area, the land is fertile and crops, such as fruits and walnuts, are cultivated. p.16, 18, 19, 62, 76

Kurd

Iran

Cameroon

Cameroon is known as "Africa in miniature" because it has various climates within the region, and the cuisine is also full of variety. There has been an ongoing conflict mostly between the country's English-speaking and French-speaking regions. p.36, 68, 70

Iran

The official language of Iran is Persian and the state religion is Shia Islam. Their dishes are unique and often use pomegranate and roses. Freedom of expression, assembly and religion are severely restricted. p.46, 82, 86

Cameroon

Ethiopia

Uganda

D.R. Congo

Democratic Republic of the Congo (D.R. Congo)

Due to the abundance of fish in the Congo River and lakes, fish is a staple part of the local diet. Varieties of grains, potatoes and corn are also available. In addition to the conflicts between neighboring countries, people continue to flee from violence even after the change of administration in 2019. p.30, 32

Uganda

Uganda is located in a tropical region on the equator. The principal foods are bananas and corn flour. The freedom of sexual minorities and political activists are severely restricted. p.28, 74

Ethiopia

The official language of Ethiopia is Amharic. Located in a high altitude, they have a unique cuisine that combines injera, a type of bread resembling a crepe, and wat, meaning stew. Social unrest has occurred due to conflicts between ethnic groups and political activities. Even now, riots occur that claim many lives due to the unstable social situation. p.56, 58, 59, 60, 61

Pakistan

Pakistan is an extremely diverse country with over 60 languages spoken. Although the state religion is Islam, there are many conflicts between various sects, ethnic and political groups.

p.48, 80, 88

Nepal

Although Nepal is a country with many ethnic groups and languages, the people share a common cuisine of a combination of curry, rice and pickles. Many people fled from political confusion in the country after it was released from the oppression of the monarchy.

p.14, 24, 42

Bangladesh

Bangladesh is rich in water resources, including the Ganges River, and fish are a staple food. It is one of the largest rice consumers in the world. The country has societal confusion due to animosities between political, ethnic and religious groups.

p.26, 34

Pakistan

Nepal

Bangladesh

Myanmar/
Burma

Sri Lanka

Myanmar/Burma

Myanmar is made up of the Burmese people and various other ethnic groups. Many people left the country due to persecution by the prolonged military regime aimed at democratic activists and minority groups. Also, the persecution against Rohingya people has drawn international attention to this day.

Burmese

The Burmese people make up about 70% of Myanmar's population. Many of them are Buddhist.   p.52, 78, 90

Kachin

The Kachin people live in mountainous region near the border of China and India. The flavours in its cuisine have been influenced by both countries. The majority of this group is Christian.   p.44, 72

Karen

The Karen people make up about 7% of Myanmar (Burma)'s population. They eat freshwater fish caught in the Salween River, which originates in Tibet. p.38, 40, 92

Chin

The Chin people live at an altitude of 3,000m and traditionally eat millet and corn. The majority of the population is Christian.   p.10, 54, 84

Sri Lanka

Sri Lanka is an island country in the Indian Ocean and has developed its own special cuisine that uses many spices by virtue of its trade and surrounding countries. Many people were forced to leave the country due to conflicts and political confusion between the Sinhalese people, who make up 70% of Sri Lanka's population, and the Tamil minority group.   p.22, 50

Please note:
The refugees who have shared their recipes in this book did not necessarily leave their countries due to the above reasons. Information on the countries and areas above is not comprehensive, and political and social situations are subject to constant change.

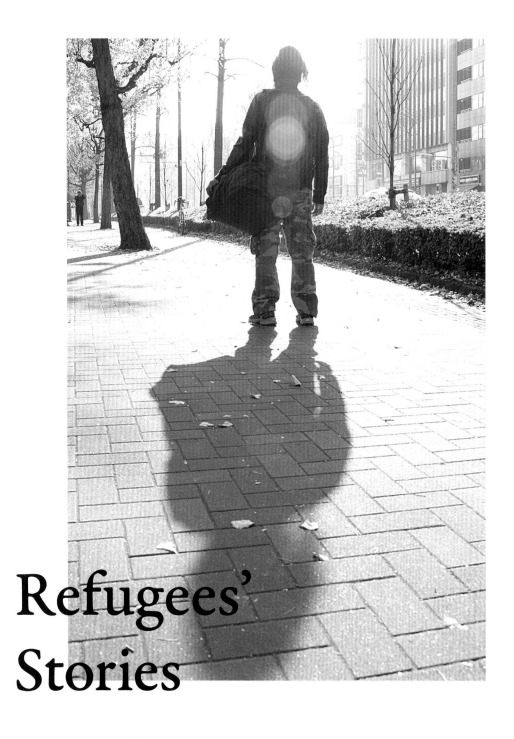

Refugees'
Stories

難民の話

息子にとってのママの味は、
私が作るクルド料理です。
もちろん、日本の料理も好きです。
特にラーメンが好き。

For my son, the taste of home
is the Kurdish dishes I make.
Of course, he also likes
Japanese food—especially ramen!

クルド出身・女性

ドルマやキョフテの作り方は、13歳ぐらいの時お母さんから教えてもらいました。結婚したら家族と一緒に食べるようにと。

日本で小学生になる息子と二人で暮らしています。クルド料理はよく作ります。息子にとってのママの味は、私が作るクルド料理です。もちろん、日本の料理も好きです。特にラーメンが好き。

今は難民申請中なので生活は大変です。先が見えなくて不安な気持ちになることもあります。

でも、クルド料理を作る時は気分が明るくなります。クルドのこと、小さかった時のことを思い出します。

味の決め手であるサルチャは叔母がクルドから送ってくれます。段ボール箱を開ける時は、幸せな気持ちになります。

料理を教えるのは、とても楽しいです。もっと日本の人にクルドのことを知ってもらいたいです。

Female from Kurd

When I was about 13 years old, my mother taught me how to make Dolma and Kofte. She told me to cook for my family once I got married.

I live in Japan with my son, who is a primary school student. I often make Kurdish food at home.

For my son, the taste of home is the Kurdish dishes I make. Of course, he also likes Japanese food—especially ramen!

Our life is difficult and unpredictable, as we are still in the process of applying for refugee status. Often, we feel anxious about our uncertain future.

Making Kurdish food, however, gives me great joy. It reminds me of my home and of my childhood in my home country.

Salcasi (tomato paste), the most crucial seasoning for Kurdish food, is sent from my aunt back home. I feel very happy as I open the delivered package.

When I sometimes teach Kurdish cooking, I truly enjoy it. I would like to see more Japanese people getting to know about Kurd.

アゼリ出身・男性

料理には、歴史があり、文化がある。だから料理を作っていると、昔同じ土地で暮らしていた人のことを思い出す。

7歳の時から、母親が作るのを見ながら学んできた。母もまた、その母から学んできた。代々受け継いできて今がある。

言葉で人を幸せにすることは、あまりできないと思う。でも、美味しい料理を食べている人の表情をみると、幸せな気持ちかどうか、わかる。

日本に逃れてきて、20年。

独裁政権の支配に抵抗し、少数民族として政治活動に参加していた。言論の自由はなかった。何度も政府に逮捕され、ついに、身の危険を感じ、逃れざるを得なかった。

まだ、母国には帰れない。できるならば、今すぐにでも戻りたい。そして、母国にいる母や兄弟と一緒に、食卓を囲みたい。

Male from Azeri

Cooking tells us about a country's history and culture. As I cook, I am reminded of the people from my own community.

When I was seven years old, I started to learn how to cook by watching my mother. She also learnt it by watching her mother. Cooking has been passed on through the generations.

I think it's difficult to make someone happy through words. But I can tell whether they are happy if I look at their faces as they eat good food.

Twenty years has passed since I escaped to Japan.

As a member of an ethnic minority in my country, I was politically active and rebelled against the dictatorship. I could not enjoy any freedom of speech. I was arrested multiple times by the government. I knew my life was in danger. I had no choice but to leave the country to seek asylum.

I haven't been able to find a way to return to my country yet. If I could, I would love to return. Then, I would sit at the dinner table with my mother and brothers once again.

ビルマ料理レストラン情報

ルビー

東京都豊島区高田3-8-5
セントラル早稲田101
Tel：03-6907-3944

Burmese Restaurant Information

Ruby

101 Central Waseda, 3-8-5 Takada,
Toshima-ku, Tokyo
Tel: 03-6907-3944

ミャンマー（ビルマ）出身・女性

　母国で民主化活動に参加していた夫は、身を守るために、ひとり、日本へ逃れざるを得ませんでした。7年間離ればなれでしたが、夫が難民認定を得ることができ、やっと、日本で再会することができました。

　母国では高校教師でしたが、日本に来てからは、希望する仕事に出合うことはできず、「それならば自分で」と、ビルマ料理のお店を始めることにしました。

　実は、料理はあまりやったことがなかったので、日本に来てから、同胞の知り合いに教えてもらいました。昔食べた母の味を再現することが難しく、試行錯誤の連続でした。

　お店は、話すこと、聞くこと、食べることがたくさんある場所。ビルマの人も、日本の人も楽しいことばかりではありません。一人で、寂しい思い、悲しい思いをしている人も、たくさんいます。

　お店があるから、いろんな人と出会うことができました。

　もちろん、母国に帰りたい気持ちはいつもあります。でも、日本でお店を始めて、国のことを聞かれたり、話したりするチャンスをもらったことはうれしく思います。

Female from Myanmar (Burma)

　My husband was a member of a democratic activist group in Myanmar (Burma). In order to protect his life, he fled to Japan alone.

　We had been separated for seven years before he received refugee status. At last, we were reunited in Japan.

　I used to be a high school teacher in my home country. In Japan, I was not able to find a job that I wanted. Instead, I thought: "Why not start my own business?" So, I opened my own Burmese restaurant.

　To tell the truth, I had never cooked very much! I asked friends in my ethnic community to teach me the basics of Burmese cooking. Through trials and errors, I struggled to replicate the taste of homemade Burmese dishes that I used to eat when I was a child.

　My restaurant is filled with people talking, listening and eating. Not everyone, including Burmese and Japanese, are always happy. Sometimes there are lonely and sad people here too.

　My restaurant brought together a variety of people.

　Of course, I still miss my home country. But I am grateful that I had a chance to start a restaurant where I can share my story with people who are interested in learning about my country.

What is a
Refugee?

難民とは?

難民とは?

「難民」。

テレビや新聞を通じて聞きなれた言葉ですが、遠い国の難民キャンプにいる人たちだけを指す言葉ではありません。

紛争や人権侵害などやむを得ず自分が生まれ育った国を逃れた人を「難民」といいます。たとえば、民主化活動に参加したことや、改宗したこと、同性を好きになったことなどが理由で、迫害を受ける人がいます。そんな難民が、日本にも逃れてきています。

日本に逃れて来る理由は様々ですが、行き先を決める時間も選択の余地も限られている場合がほとんどです。なかには、平和で安全な国だと思った、地理的に近かった、ビザが最初に下りた国がたまたま日本だった、という理由で日本を目指す人もいます。

しかし、迫害を逃れてたどり着いた日本で直面するのは、厳しい現実です。

日本語や日本の法律は分からない。家も、仕事もなく、頼りにできる存在もない。難民として日本政府に認めてもらうための手続きは厳しく、難民認定される人は非常に限られています。近年では、毎年約1万人が日本で難民申請をしますが、認められるのは数十名に留まっています。また手続きも長期間かかり、平均で約4年、長い場合は10年以上待っている人もいます。生活基盤や法的地位が不安定な状況の中、一人ひとり、様々な困難を乗り越えながら、日本社会で暮らしています。

What is a Refugee?

Refugee.

You may have heard this word through world news, on the TV or in a newspaper. You may think this term only applies to those in refugee camps in a distant country.

In fact, a refugee is a person who had no other choice but to escape from their home country to protect his or her life from conflict or persecution. For example, people who flee their country out of fear of being persecuted for their pro-democratic activities, faith or sexuality are considered refugees. Those people are coming to Japan to seek asylum.

There are various reasons for their arrival here, but in most cases, they have limited choices and little time to make their destination. Some choose Japan thinking it is a peaceful and safe country, some choose Japan for its geographic proximity, others because a visa was granted quicker than from other countries.

However, escaping from persecution and finally reaching Japan does not lead to the peaceful new life that they dreamed of.

Understanding the Japanese language and laws are challenging. The process for applying for refugee status is difficult. The Japanese government issues very few. In recent years, about 10,000 people apply for the refugee application every year, but only dozens are approved. It is also a lengthy process. On average, it takes about four years, but can take ten years or more for refugee status to be determined. With no living or legal assurance, each refugee and people seeking asylum overcome various obstacles and be a part of Japanese society.

About M4R

M4Rについて

Meal for Refugees（以下 M4R）は日本に暮らす難民の故郷の味を学生食堂で展開、「食」を通じて難民を知る・支える活動です。学生と認定NPO法人 難民支援協会（JAR）が共同で行っています。

M4Rメニューは『海を渡った故郷の味 Flavours Without Borders（2013年版）』がもとになっています。売り上げの一部は、JARへ寄付され、難民支援に活用されます。2013年の発足からこれまでに全国の40を超える大学・高校で導入、約11万食を売り上げ、160万円以上の寄付金になりました。社食、レストランなどでも実施されています。

Meal for Refugees (M4R) is a program which gives the refugees' living in Japan a taste of home. M4R is staffed by students and Japan Association for Refugees (JAR) who get to know and help support these refugees through food. The menu of M4R is based on "Flavours Without Borders" (2013 version). Part of the proceeds from the meals will be donated to JAR and be used to support refugees living in Japan. Since M4R started in 2013, over 40 universities and high schools in Japan have been introduced to the project. M4R has sold approximately one hundred ten thousand meals, which amounts to a contribution of 1.6 million yen. M4R activities are conducted in school and company cafeterias and restaurants.

What students are saying

学生の声

学生が主体となって、学食から気軽に難民問題を発信できることに魅力を感じ、M4Rの活動に取り組んでいます！

We are fascinated by M4R, which is mainly driven by students, we work on M4R activities and can offer help to the refugee's conveniently using the school's cafeteria.

M4Rは難民問題に関して「何かしたい」を「カタチ」にできる活動です！　全国のM4Rメンバーと同じ目標に向かって活動ができることも魅力の一つです。

With M4R, we can turn our ideas into reality to help Japan's refugees. Another attraction is that with M4R, all the members from different parts of the countries can work towards the same goals.

制作協力者からのメッセージ

「難民」という立場の方と会うのは初めての事だったので、どう接したらいいか見当もつきませんでしたが、お目にかかった方は皆さん、こちらを包み込むようなあたたかな瞳を持った方ばかりでした。その彼らの自国を愛し懐かしむ心のつまった料理、故郷の風景が目に浮かぶような鮮やかな色彩と華やかな香りをこの写真で少しでもお伝えできれば幸せです。

矢田堀 喜久代

もし、私たちが日本を離れ外国で暮らすことになったら、どんな故郷の味や母の味を思い出すでしょう。きっと、肉ジャガや唐揚げ、カレーライスやハンバーグといった家族で食べた何気ない日々の料理を思い出すのではないでしょうか。難民の方々にも、大切な家族と囲んだ食卓があったはずです。家族の笑顔が溢れる食事のひと時があったはずです。彼らが愛する家族と笑顔で食卓を囲む日が、再び訪れることを願わずにはいられません。

小梶 さとみ

撮影を担当させてもらった、難民の女性は、材料の分量も調理の時間、タイミングもからだが覚えているという感じで、あっというまに料理ができあがっていきました。一回つくったら、からだが覚えたくなるレシピたちだと思います。

齊藤 亜樹

料理を作り一緒に食べている時、皆さんとても楽しそうな顔をしていました。このプロジェクトを通じて出会った方々は皆、日本での生活を受入れながらも、それぞれのルーツと深いつながりを持っていました。材料や調理方法が違っていても、おいしい料理は国を超えて理解されるものです。大きく異なるバックグラウンドを持った人々の間でさえ、料理というものはすぐに楽しい話題になりますし、そこからまた、深い話をするきっかけにもなります。

アントニー・トラン

撮影は、異国の方と一緒に異国の料理を作ったり食べたりと、とても楽しいひと時でした。異国の料理は普段食べている食事とは全然違って、新鮮でしたし、やはり料理という世界共通の切り口から、難民問題を考えるというのはとても素敵な企画だと思いました。

山城 由

Messages from the contributors

When I first met refugees, I had no idea how to interact with them. However, all those I met had a deep sense of warmth and welcomed me whole-heartedly. I hope my photos of the dishes can communicate their deep longing for their homeland and that the vivid colours and rich flavours of the dishes will stir your imagination to picture the beautiful scenery of their country.

Kikuyo Yatabori

If I were forced to leave Japan and start a life abroad, what tastes or home cooking would I miss the most? Surely, I would be reminded of the simple taste of family meals, such as stewed beef and potatoes, fried chicken with soy sauce, curry rice or Japanese-style meatloaf. In the same way, the refugees must have enjoyed their precious family meals with joy and peace. I cannot help but pray for the refugees to be able to share meals together with their families once again.

Satomi Kokaji

During the photo shoot, I was impressed by a female refugee who seemed to be cooking a dish from memory. She cooked so quickly, as if her body knew exactly the right amount of ingredients and timing! If you give it a try once, then your body will want to remember the recipe.

Aki Saito

I saw a lot of joy on everybody's faces during the preparation and sharing of these meals. All the people I met during this project remained deeply connected to their roots, while also embracing their life in Japan. No matter how different the ingredients or the methods of cooking may be, good food is something that is universally appreciated. Even between people from radically different backgrounds, cooking instantly becomes a subject of happy discussions and even often leads to deeper topics.

Antony Tran

At the photo shoot, I truly enjoyed cooking and eating a variety of ethnic food with the people from different countries. All the ethnic dishes I tried were totally different from what I usually eat. I thought that this was a great project to think about the issue of refugees through the universally shared topic of food.

Yui Yamashiro

制作協力者一覧（2013）

マッコーリー・グループ・ジャパン
資金提供・制作協力

カスタムメディア株式会社
編集・デザイン

アグネス・ペトルシオン
翻訳

アントニー・トラン
撮影（表紙, p.36, 37, 56-61, 68-70, 75）

飯塚　明夫
撮影（p.44, 72）

池田　なつき
翻訳

岡本　ありさ
制作協力、翻訳

スチュワート& カレン・スマイス
制作協力

小梶　さとみ
校正

小島　優香
制作協力、翻訳

齊藤　亜樹
撮影（p.10, 84, 85）

嶋　倫子
制作協力、翻訳、撮影（p.14-19, 24, 25, 30, 32, 33, 35, 38-43, 53-55, 62, 63, 67, 76, 81, 82, 92, 105）

スコット・コズグリフ
翻訳

矢田堀　喜久代
撮影（p.12, 20, 28, 48, 52, 64, 66, 71, 74, 78, 80, 88, 90, 100）

山城　由（Surmometer Inc.）
ディレクション（p.10, 84, 85）

矢野　津々美
撮影（p.18, 98）

株式会社プロントコーポレーション
会場提供

日本福音ルーテル社団
会場提供

List of Contributors (2013)

Macquarie Group Japan
Sponsorship, production

Custom Media K.K.
Editing, design

Agnes Petrucione
Translation

Antony Tran
Photography (Cover, p.36, 37, 56-61, 68-70, 75)

Akio Iizuka
Photography (p.44, 72)

Natsuki Ikeda
Translation

Alisa Okamoto
Production, translation

Stuart & Karen Smythe
Production

Satomi Kokaji
Emendation

Yuuka Kojima
Production, translation

Aki Saito
Photography (p.10, 84, 85)

Michiko Shima
Production, translation, photography (p.14-19, 24, 25, 30, 32, 33, 35, 38-43, 53-55, 62, 63, 67, 76, 81, 82, 92, 105)

Scott Cosgriff
Translation

Kikuyo Yatabori
Photography(p.12, 20, 28, 48, 52, 64, 66, 71, 74, 78, 80, 88, 90, 100)

Yui Yamashiro (Surmometer Inc.)
Direction (p.10, 84, 85)

Tsutsumi Yano
Photography (p.18, 98)

Pronto Corporation
Venue

The Japan Evangelical Lutheran Association
Venue

認定NPO法人 難民支援協会 (JAR) について

1999年設立。紛争や迫害により故郷を追われ、日本へ逃れてきた難民が安心して暮らせることを目指して活動する。難民申請の手続きや、来日直後の緊急期を含む医食住の支援、自立に向けた就労支援などの直接支援に加えて、地域社会との橋渡しや、政策提言、認知啓発など多様な関係者への働きかけにも力を入れている。年間の支援対象者の出身国は約60か国にわたり、来訪相談者数は約600人、相談件数は4,000件以上(2021年度実績)。
国連難民高等弁務官事務所(UNHCR)駐日事務所のパートナー団体。

日本に逃れてきた難民を支えるためのご寄付は難民支援協会で受け付けております。
皆さまのご支援をお願いいたします。

www.refugee.or.jp / Tel: 03-5379-6001

About Japan Association for Refugees (JAR)

JAR was established in 1999 to support refugees who have fled to Japan due to conflict and persecution. JAR's goal is to ensure that refugees are safe and can settle down in a new land with hope. JAR provides comprehensive assistance for individual refugees by supporting the refugee application procedure, providing food, shelter, medical assistance, and job assistance. JAR also collaborates with various groups in local communities, conducts advocacy, and raises awareness. JAR supports refugees from over 60 countries, providing consultation for 600 individuals and more than 4,000 cases per year (FY 2021). JAR is an Implementing Partner of the United Nations High Commissioner for Refugees (UNHCR) in Japan.

If you would like to make a donation to help refugees in Japan, please visit the website at

www.refugee.or.jp/en/ or call +81-3-5379-6001.

デザイン	天池　聖（drnco.）
制作協力	黒川　英和
制作協力	高木　悠磨
翻訳協力	中込　幸子
翻訳協力	トレナマン　真弓
編集	酒井　美奈子
編集	浅見　英治

Design	Hijiri Amaike (drnco.)
Production	Hidekazu Kurokawa
Production	Yuma Takagi
Translation	Sachiko Nakagome
Translation	Mayumi Trenaman
Editing	Minako Sakai
Editing	Eiji Asami

海を渡った故郷の味 新装版
Flavours Without Borders　new edition

2020年2月1日初版発行
2023年5月31日2刷発行

編　　著	認定NPO法人 難民支援協会
発 行 者	後藤佑介
発 行 所	株式会社トゥーヴァージンズ
	東京都千代田区九段北4-1-3
	Tel:03-5212-7442　Fax:03-5212-7889
	https://www.twovirgins.jp

| 印刷・製本 | 藤原印刷株式会社 |

ISBN 978-4-908406-53-9
©Japan Association for Refugees 2020, Printed in Japan